THE LEGENDARY LITTLE MOTORCYCLES

SUPER CUB
DAX
MONKEY

Gerfried Vogt-Möbs

4880 Lower Valley Road • Atglen, PA 19310

About the Author:
Gerfried Vogt-Möbs is an experienced writer and motor journalist with deep contacts and knowledge in the scene.

Translated from the German by David Johnston.
Originally published as *Little Honda: Die Legendären Kleinmotorräder*, © 2021 Delius Klasing Verlag, Bielefeld

Library of Congress Control Number: 2022944423

Text: Gerfried Vogt-Möbs
Layout: Jörg Weusthoff, Weusthoff & Reiche Design, Hamburg
Cover design: Christopher Bower
Type set in Univers LT Std/Swift LT Pro

ISBN: 978-0-7643-6582-9
Printed in China

Published by Schiffer Publishing, Ltd.
4880 Lower Valley Road
Atglen, PA 19310
Phone: (610) 593-1777; Fax: (610) 593-2002
Email: info@schifferbooks.com
Web: www.schifferbooks.com

Schiffer Publishing's titles are available at special discounts for bulk purchases for sales promotions or premiums. Special editions, including personalized covers, corporate imprints, and excerpts, can be created in large quantities for special needs. For more information, contact the publisher.

Photo credits:
Honda Motor Company: advertising material, ads, catalogs
H. Kemp: pp. 4–5
J. Gassebner: p. 39 (*bottom*), p. 63
C. Leavey: p. 43
G. Schumacher: p. 44, p. 47, p. 48, p. 49, pp. 50–51, p. 53 (*top*)
J. Sijses: pp. 68–69
C. Wimmer: p. 80 (*left*)
K. van Oostrum: p. 116, p. 173, p. 176
M. Engels: p. 124, p. 125
S. Wolf: p. 133, p. 152
G. Rotter: pp. 138–139, p. 141, p. 145
J. Haidle: p. 141
A. Mesecke: p. 142
D. Biene: p. 145
S. Zollinger: p. 145, pp. 148–149
T. Disch: p. 147
O. Blaubach: p. 150, p. 151
S. Berthold: p. 174
Dove/Getty Images: p. 184
All other photographs: Archive G. Vogt-Möbs

PACK MULES FOR EGGS, PIG CARCASS HALVES, GOLDFISH, TORPEDOES, AND EVEN COFFINS: FOR PEOPLE IN SOUTHEAST ASIA, THE SUPER CUB HAS BEEN ONE OF THE MOST IMPORTANT MEANS OF TRANSPORT FOR MORE THAN HALF A CENTURY.

Q.5
ĐT : 8567680 - 8575387
VĂN PHÒNG ĐẠI DIỆN
Quận 5
73A
ĐT:8567680
8575387
ĐẠI LỘC
HONDA

HONDAS A-TEAM:
THE Z 50 A WAS THE IDEAL VEHICLE, AND NOT JUST AS A PIT BIKE IN THE PIT LANE OR FOR PHOTOGRAPHERS.

ホンダNEWモンキーZ50Z

MAKING THE CASE THAT IT BELONGS IN EVERY HOUSEHOLD, THERE WERE INNOVATIVE ADVERTISEMENTS IN *LIFE* AND *READER'S DIGEST* PROMOTING THE LITTLE HONDA MOTORCYCLES AS A FAMILY THING. ANYONE COULD RIDE IT, EVEN WITHOUT LEATHER GEAR AND THE BIKER IMAGE.

ine

VERSATILITY: WITH SMALL WHEELS, DEEP STEP-THROUGH DESIGNS, OFF-ROAD DESIGN, OR GENTLEMANLIKE STYLING, HONDA MADE THE ENTRY-LEVEL CLASS INTERESTING TO EVERYONE BY OFFERING AN ENORMOUS RANGE OF DIFFERENT LOOKS.

CONTENTS

Thai
HONDA

FORE-WORD

A MILLION SELLER— HONDA'S CASH COW

The influence of motorized vehicles on the development of humankind can hardly be overestimated. The small-motorcycle sector's major role in this progress became clear only after World War II. Soichiro Honda gleaned as much information as possible from European manufacturers, but he then used this knowledge to develop something completely new—and achieved what no other motorcycle manufacturer had managed before or since. His original model, the C 100 Super Cub, became a global success, which he continued to refine. On this basis, his team created an extensive range of practical as well as unique vehicles. On the one hand, they were able to stand out with their sophisticated technology, high quality, and cheeky design, and on the other hand, they were able to meet the needs of many fringe groups—which had no interest in high-powered motorcycles or speed records—in an inexpensive, stylish, and practical way. Of course, Honda also served the racing circuit—but the money for this was ultimately earned by its small four stroke machines, the "bee's knees," as the British so nicely put it. The Honda Cub also functioned as a "worker bee" in developing countries; photographer Hans Kemp portrayed this reality in his impressive book titled *Bikes of Burden*.

On the following pages, I would like to show you just how flexibly and imaginatively Honda's little machines muscled their way into all the world's markets. In view of the abundance of variations, the focus of this book is less on exhaustive technical explanations and endless specifications of the mini motorcycles, but rather on the company's clever advertising and the multilayered development, to which the European nations of Belgium, Netherlands, and Luxembourg made a decisive contribution.

I would like to thank all the photographers, guest authors, and collectors without whom this book would not have been possible: Marjin Engels, Gilles Schumacher, Claire Leavey, Stefan Wolf, Jürgen Gassebner, Thomas Schinagl, Peter Lerch, Daniela Göckeritz, Dr. Thomas Becker, Thomas Disch, Stefan Berthold, Tom Haanstra, Joop Sijses, and Kjell van Oostrum, as well as Jürgen Haidle, Georg Rotter, and all other Honda enthusiasts who helped me

I'd like to close with a gas station (economy) joke by my esteemed colleague Frank-Albert Illg: "Fill it up, please," says the Honda Cub driver with his seat folded up and pointing to the tank. "With pleasure," the gas station attendant replies succinctly. "Would you like me to cough into your tires too?" I hope you enjoy reading and discovering, and that you always have a clean oil filter centrifuge.

Gerfried Vogt-Möbs

スーパーカブ
C 100
C 102
HONDA MOTOR CO., LTD.

ONE FOR ALL

The ingenious idea: one-handed driving, trouble-free operation, inexpensive, and as low maintenance as possible.

SIMPLE, UNCOMPLICATED, ECONOMICAL, AND NO ANNOYING TWO-STROKE ENGINE: AFTER ITS EXPERIENCE WITH THE CUB F, WITH ITS "CLIP-ON" GASOLINE ENGINE ON ITS REAR WHEEL, IT WAS CLEAR AS DAY TO HONDA THAT ONLY A VEHICLE WITH A FOUR-STROKE ENGINE COULD BE SUCCESSFUL IN THE LONG TERM.

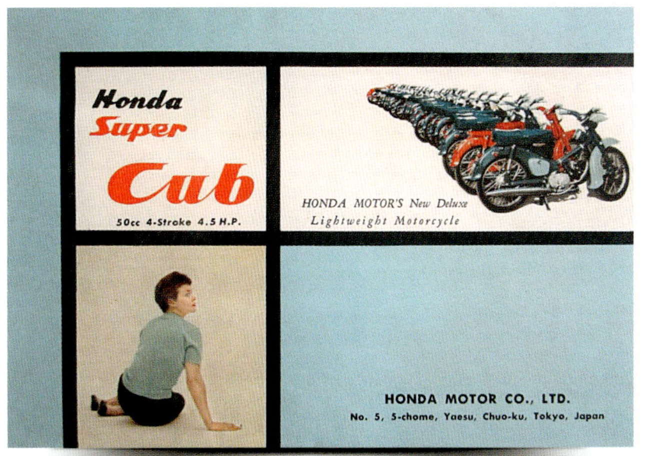

Women in particular were expected to get along well with the Cub—that's why they were put in the spotlight in early advertisements.

HONDA
スーパーカブ
スポーツカブ
50.55

世界一をお選び下さい

ホンダはかつてのオートバイ王国フランスの生産量を上廻る一日4000台、月10万台のホンダ製品を世界に送りだす、まさに質量ともに世界一のオートバイメーカーです。

新しい乗物のエース……〈スーパーカブ・スポーツカブ〉はこのクラスでは余りにもぜいたくな性能とスタイルをもつ車として、皆様に使われ愛されて5年を迎え、世界の人々のくらしのテンポの中にとけこみ250万の人々に新たな〈能率〉と〈楽しみ〉を知っていただきました。

An ideal team: Soichiro Honda and Takeo Fujisawa complemented each other perfectly. The two were united by ambition—but also diligence and foresight.

A PERFECT PAIRING SPARKS A NEW BEGINNING

He was restless but determined; Soichiro Honda was a mechanic, doer, inventor, thinker, and aesthete. He was also a sensitive person, a great optimist, and a fan of fast machines. He met Takeo Fujisawa four years after the end of World War II. The two complemented each other perfectly, which can be seen as the economic cornerstone of their vehicle empire, which would never have come into being without the Super Cub.

As early as 1947, the then-forty-one-year-old Honda returned to design work, having given up his company—which made piston rings—and selling it to Toyota. After the war, mobility was once again in demand, and the newly founded Honda Motor Company was aiming to fill this niche—with a 50 cc, two-stroke engine that could be mounted as a kit on the rear wheel of a bicycle. The thing was not exactly reliable, however—nor was the company's first complete motorcycle, which was manufactured and sold as the Type D starting in 1949. Each week, the small Honda team managed to complete just twenty-five machines, but its output soon tripled. Customers quickly recognized the advantages of having a network of dealerships where they could have their machines serviced and repaired—a first success for Fujisawa, who, operating in the company background as a marketing expert, pulled the strings on sales strategies while Soichiro single-mindedly tinkered with new vehicle ideas. Honda soon decided to turn his back on the two-stroke engine with the deflector piston that was common at the time, and he hoped that the Honda Dream would live up to its name and satisfy customer demands for less noise and less exhaust odor. Honda and Kiyochi Kawashima developed a four-stroke engine, which even had an overhead camshaft as the icing on the cake. With its 150 cc single-cylinder engine, the motorcycle was first produced in 1951 and rolled off the production line 36,000 times by 1953.

Even when the name still stood for Honda's two-stroke auxiliary engine, Cub already meant "Cheap Urban Bike." The Cub F (*above*) was the first Honda sales success, available only as a kit, and was discontinued in 1954. The Model A, also an installation kit for bicycles with a belt drive to the rear wheel, was created in 1947. The small engine with a deflector piston produced 0.5 hp at 5,000 rpm.

Honda's Juno K in a contemporaneous advertisement. Unfortunately, the scooter, which was produced for only a short time, could not fly.

Lambretta authority and scooter collector Vittorio Tessera in Milan is one of the few Europeans who own a Juno K. The fairing was completely made of aluminum, like those on German vehicles.

A FLOP LEADS TO NEW IDEAS

The Korean War brought about an economic boom in Japan. Demand increased, and whether the partners of the young motorcycle company wanted it or not, the company's production facilities had to be modernized in order to work faster and more economically. As early as 1951, Honda introduced a new company philosophy called the "three joys": manufacture, sell, and acquire. The Type E, which had a pressed-steel frame similar to German models and the Danish Nimbus, became the first Honda motorcycle to be exported to the United States. While motorcycle sales in Europe plummeted thanks to the German economic miracle (Wirtschaftswunder), in Japan the same thing happened when the economy weakened again.

The elaborate Juno K, designed as an unrivaled luxury scooter, turned out to be a flop because of its technical immaturity. What was Honda to do next?

Looking back, the company founder later explained, "For the first time, there were dissatisfied customers. And they were right." With backing from the banks, Fujisawa and Honda came up with a master plan. They would modernize from the bottom up: the two-stroke Cub kits would be discontinued and replaced. To score points in markets such as the US and Europe, success in motorsports was necessary. Together, the two planned a trip to Europe to explore the market and also to gain inspiration; company visits to long-established manufacturers such as NSU, Zündapp, and Puch, they agreed, could perhaps help the Honda company get off the ground through strategic partnerships.

Compared to the Cub F, the new motorcycle was to have a more respectable performance—basically combining serviceability with ease of handling, so that every member of the family could operate it. "Even before they left, we had to put two prototypes on wheels," explained Yoshiro Harada, then head of frame engineering design. He had been appointed overall project manager at that time. "The two of them came home with five motorcycles in their luggage," he recalled. Immediately upon their return, a meeting was called, during which Honda drew his ideas on the floor in chalk. "When he shouted, 'The engine will be a four-stroke,' the employees who surrounded him weren't at all surprised," continued Harada. "They all knew that by then he really hated two-stroke engines. In early 1957, we started development, which began with design of the engine."

50 CC FOUR-STROKE: A CHALLENGE

Entrusted with the task of team leader was Daiji Hoshino, who had been with Honda since 1951. Hoshino had experience with steam engines and had previously worked on the further developed two-stroke Cub Type F. "No one would have chosen a four-stroke engine with a displacement of just 50 cc as a series product; it was no easy task. Every day he [Honda] came to me in the design office and looked over my shoulder as I did the calculations. It was worse when we started with drawings – he could read drawings quickly and comment on or correct them just as quickly," recalled Hoshino. Since the engine was to be installed horizontally, heat generation was a major problem. It was therefore decided to add cooling holes in the cast-iron cylinder head, which then produced the desired results. "Power output, too, was rather modest, but this was a 50 cc engine, so the surface area available in the cylinder head was too small," Hoshino explained. "If we used standard 12 mm diameter spark plugs, we couldn't increase the diameter of the valves. We decided to take a bold step and use 10 mm plugs." Or, in Soichiro Honda's words, "Common sense is there in order for us to break through it. NGK, the plug manufacturer, was very positive about developing 10 mm plugs. We got an output of 4.3 PS, so we ended up with about twice as much power as anybody else."

IT COULDN'T BE SIMPLER TO DRIVE—PREFERABLY WITH ONE HAND

Food delivery services are not just a phenomenon of the twenty-first century. With "noodle stores" already a trend in Japan in the mid-1950s, Soichiro Honda was inspired to expand the specifications of the new vehicle accordingly in front of the assembled team: "It has to be simple. So that the delivery boy can balance the tray on one hand and accelerate with the other. In other words, the clutch shouldn't be operated by hand." Even the Dream, the Type D, did not have a clutch lever – and a centrifugal clutch seemed the best solution for the new one as well. While Akira Akima supervised the testing, the ideal solution was selected from eight different ideas. The foot shift lever and actuating mechanism, similar to those on the Type D, were suitable for declutching and changing gears.

"We gave it our best effort, and it worked flawlessly right away," recalled Akima. In June, Kinchinosuke Ando joined the team as the person with overall responsibility for the frame and add-on components. He calculated the center of gravity, seat layout, and weight distribution. Although the short swing arm from Nakajima's pen turned out to be much more delicate and narrower than that of any previous vehicle, the solution was still robust enough to handle bad roads. "The frame structure was already finished when I started, and the clay model with 17-inch wheels was just in the works. But what

From an early stage, there were various color and equipment options for both the C 100 and the sporty C 110.

surprised me the most was that we had no blueprints with length, width, steering-head angle, or caster measurements to use as a template. Normally you had something like that as a basis—but we did it the other way around," recalled Ando. One parameter, however, was important to Honda: weight could not exceed 55 kilograms (about 121 pounds). Fortunately, materials such as polyethylene had just been developed, and manufacturing technologies were making great strides.

The Dream D from 1949, with box frame and backflow scavenging à la those employed by German motorcycle manufacturer Ardie.

THE 100 CC ENGINE, A COMPACT UNIT WITH CLEVERLY DESIGNED TECHNOLOGY. AS IT TURNED OUT, HOWEVER, VERY ROUGH HANDLING COULD BREAK THE KICK-STARTER SHAFT.

The Incomparable Four-Stroke Engine

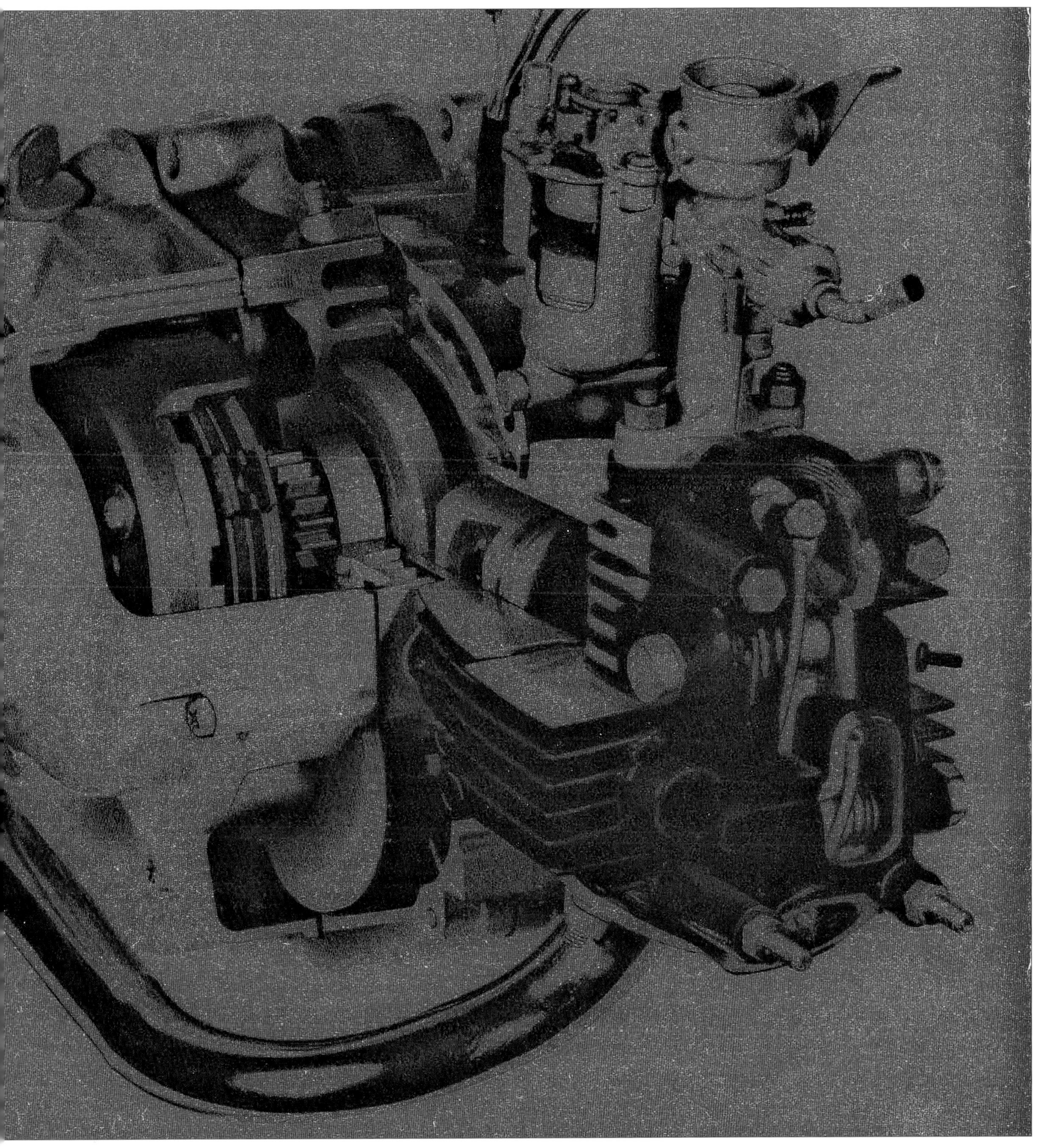

A true global player: Ten million of the small Honda standout had been sold by 1973. It was offered in 160 countries.

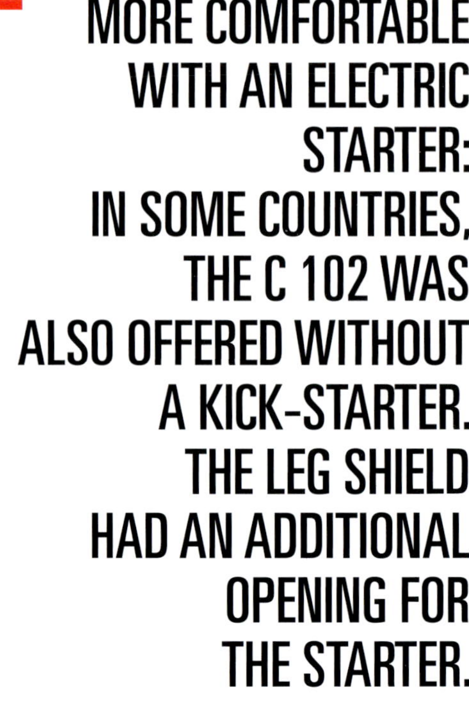

MORE COMFORTABLE WITH AN ELECTRIC STARTER: IN SOME COUNTRIES, THE C 102 WAS ALSO OFFERED WITHOUT A KICK-STARTER. THE LEG SHIELD HAD AN ADDITIONAL OPENING FOR THE STARTER.

AN ABSOLUTE MUST FOR MALE AND FEMALE RIDERS

By April, "Operation Special M" was far enough along for fairing parts to take concrete shape. Here, too, a newcomer was at work: Jozaburo Kimura, who joined Honda immediately after graduating from college in November 1956. "When I was pulled off the Benly and ordered to design the Special M, Honda often said to me, 'Design something that fits in your hand.' It wasn't until I thought about it that I knew what he meant: something like a tool that anyone could easily operate without qualms or contortions."

Honda had precise ideas when it came to the step-through design. According to European ideas, the tank always sat in front of the step-through, but that didn't suit Honda, who told his team, "We also want customers who wear skirts, so we can't put the tank where it will interfere." Kimura racked his brain, then finally came up with the solution of placing the tank under the seat. Getting on and off easily was one of the key virtues of the Super Cub's styling, and admittedly this concept was a Honda maxim. In December, when the model was finally ready after eight months of work, the following took place, as described by Tarisuke Mori, another young designer:

> "Summon the managing director," Honda said to me. A surprised Fujisawa quickly emerged from his office in Yeasu, and his business partner spent about fifteen minutes explaining all the details and merits of the future machine.
>
> "What do you think?" he asked him. "How many will we be able to sell?"
>
> "Well, about 30,000," he replied impassively, without giving it a great deal of thought.
>
> I asked him, "Do you mean 30,000 a year?"
>
> "Don't be silly," Fujisawa then said. "Thirty thousand a month."

"What also dumbfounded us," recalls Kawashima, also on the engine development team, "was the fact that he had already set the net selling price—at 55,000 yen." The new Honda was to be sold by 1,500 selected dealers. The factory in Saitama was able to produce 27,000 vehicles, which was not enough, so all production of the Super Cub was moved to Suzaka starting in 1960. It soon became obvious that the new Honda was going to be a success story, because the Honda shop in Tokyo was already able to accept orders worth (the current equivalent of) about $136,000 (140,000 euros) on August 1, the day that sales of the Super Cub began.

As early as 1959, the first full year of sales, Honda produced 167,443 units. Pressed-steel frame, short swing arm, enclosed chain case—these sound today like rather modest features for the most consequential motorcycle of all. But both Honda and Fujisawa were sure that this bike would find friends worldwide. The Honda American Motor Company was launched in June 1959. This time, Honda and Fujisawa acted as visionaries; though scarcely more than 6,000 motorcycles were sold in the US at the time, they estimated potential sales of at least 80,000. "The American salesmen thought we were friendly clowns," the company boss later reported, smiling wisely.

ABARTH

HONDA'S MINI MOTORCYCLES SPREAD AROUND THE WORLD

Five speeds, but just 5.1 hp—despite its new engine, the follow-up to the C 110 was not a sales success everywhere.

WHILE THE GERMAN HONDA SUBSIDIARY INITIALLY STRUGGLED UNSUCCESSFULLY AGAINST ESTABLISHED COMPETITORS FROM KORNWESTHEIM, NUREMBERG, AND MUNICH, HONDA PLAYED OUT ITS MARKET OPPORTUNITIES IN OTHER COUNTRIES SUCH AS THE US AND THE UNITED KINGDOM—THANKS TO MUCH MORE AGGRESSIVE AND PRESENT ADVERTISING.

Recreational pleasure for him and her—the "American way of riding" was reasonably priced at just $245.

The US slogan "Honda shapes the world of wheels" was also adopted for the UK in the early 1970s.

The C 114 was advertised more frequently in England, as well as in Belgium, the Netherlands, and Luxembourg, than in Germany. Once, in 1964, the C 110 Sports Cub made it into a moped comparison test by the magazine *Hobby*.

Soichiro Honda was particularly enthusiastic about the NSU plant in Neckarsulm, Germany, and he also thought the simple but robust design of the Fox engine was ingenious. For the C 100 drive, he adopted the idea of centrifugal lubrication. Instead of an oil pump, a tiny scoop dipped into a kind of sump with each crankshaft revolution; it was constantly refilled by camshaft drive from the oil sump, which contained just 600 cc of lubricant.

Honda broke completely new ground with the automatic clutch, which utilized the torque of the 4.5 hp engine and did not provide the necessary frictional connection until just above 4,000 rpm. Another ingenious and technically interesting idea was the coupling of the three-speed transmission's clutch and gearshift lever; regardless of whether the gears were being shifted up or down, an extra operating lever disengaged the clutch even before the gear was changed. The exercise of gently engaging or disengaging the clutch via the shift lever thus became child's play.

The C 100 Super Cub was ready just in time for the Tokyo Motor Show in August 1958. It was a competitive two-wheeler with 17-inch wheels that combined the advantages of a scooter with those of a moped, a so-called Scooterette. The use of polyethylene saved a lot of weight, and thanks to the cleverly designed drive and lightweight pressed-steel frame, it was easy to ride. The C 100 heralded a turning point at Honda. Because so many orders came in, the monthly output of 30,000 vehicles soon had to be doubled – the several years of planning quickly paid off.

And what the company had only dared to hope for in its wildest dreams was achieved with the little machine at the beginning of the 1960s: thanks to a clever, nationwide advertising campaign in magazines such as *Reader's Digest*, *Life*, and *Look*, the four-stroke C 100 quickly conquered the entire US. "You meet the nicest people on a Honda" read the text that accompanied illustrations of students, housewives, and businesspeople riding Super Cubs. "Americans have fallen in love with Honda," wrote *Life* magazine, and the Beach Boys were soon singing about the beloved "Little Honda." Across the pond, the C 102 was the most popular. From 1960, it spoiled its riders as the first available 50 cc motorcycle with an electric starter! For this purpose, an 11 Ah battery was installed, and instead of the 30-watt magneto ignition, the luxury variant received a battery and coil ignition.

Typical of the Honda 50s of the time were the sweeping rectangular rearview mirrors and the extremely narrow silhouette, along with the 2.25-17-inch tires.

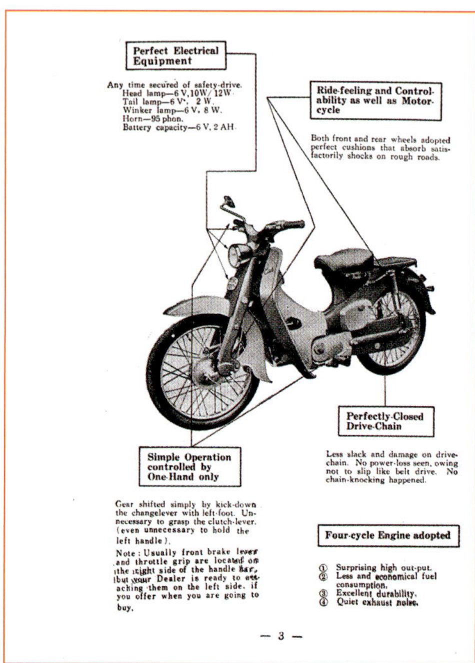

Honda's motorcycles were a hit—and not just on Valentine's Day. By the early 1960s, the original model had become a C 65 as well as a C 90. Those who wanted to drive fully automatically in England went for the PC 50 from 1968 onward.

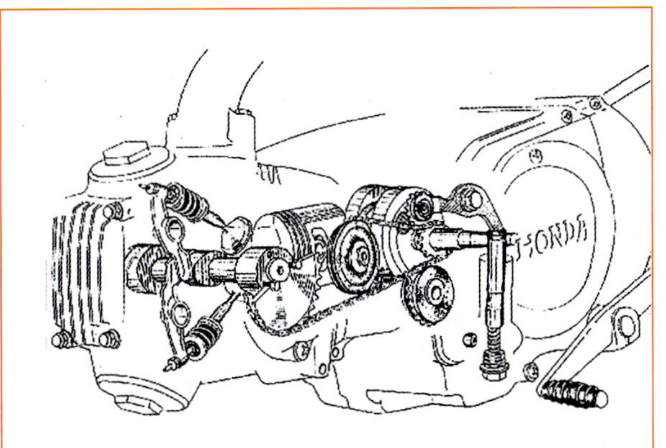

The new 50 cc OHC four-stroke was introduced in 1965. It was lighter, ran more quietly, and promised higher engine speeds for future models. Instead of centrifugal lubrication, however, an oil pump and timing-chain tensioner were now required.

France awarded the C 100 the "Mode Coupé" in October 1963 for its outstanding engineering, but in Germany the newly appointed Hamburg importer Karl-Heinz Meller soon sensed that the small Japanese machine was unfortunately no match for its domestic competitors from Kreidler, Zündapp, and Hercules. But Siegfried Rauch, head of *Das Motorrad*, was impressed by the quaint little bike and devoted four pages to it at the beginning of 1960. He singled out the Cub 50's engine and performance for special praise. "It bubbled along with a nice, even idle—and it's undeniable: irrespective of all technical arguments, the quiet four-stroke idle somehow makes a cultivated final impression, especially on such a small vehicle." His displeasure, on the other hand, was aroused by standard turn signals ("Again and again, one forgets to switch them off since they are difficult to see; fortunately they are obviously not taken seriously by other road users for the time being.") and the electrical system, which was probably too extensive by the standards of the time. "One cannot help feeling," wrote the motorcycle boss, "that the poor little alternator has been saddled with a bit too much after all." His mistrust was certainly unfounded on this point; worse was that Rauch was unfortunately completely mistaken about the sales chances of the small Super Cub in Germany. "The stronger the tendency toward ever further power increases in 50 cc engines, the greater the chances of the four-stroke should become," he had noted.

JAPANESE INDIVIDUALISM: SOMETHING FOR EVERY TASTE

It would have been nice. Meller put in a great deal of effort, and the Honda parent company paid for countless full-page advertisements. In Great Britain, Belgium, Netherlands, and Luxembourg, the C 100 sold quite well, but it was the sporty C 110 with its four-speed transmission and manual clutch, which finally looked like a real moped with its raised muffler and closed seat line, that attracted lively interest in Germany. Honda had increased the compression ratio of the engine (9.5 instead of 8.5), and the cylinder head was no longer cast from gray iron but from light alloy. The Scooterette's pushed short swing arm was also retained on the C 110 and its C 111 (automatic version with solo seat) and C 114 (four-speed version from 1963 with horizontal exhaust pipe) variants, but the pressed-steel frame was redesigned.

In the spring of 1964, the German magazine *Hobby* decided to conduct a large moped comparison test. The C 110 competed against Kreidler's Super 5, Zündapp's KS 50 S, and the Neckarsulm Quick 50. Also in the running were the Hercules K 50 and DKW's most powerful Hummel version of the Type 166. The little Japanese machine did well. It scored points for its low fuel consumption of 2.44 liters per 100 kilometers (96.4 mpg) and its low purchase price (1,045 marks). Nevertheless, it managed only second-to-last place, ahead of the NSU. The reasons were its lack of performance (73.2 kph [45.5 mph] over 1,000 meters [0.6 miles] under the most ideal conditions), but also its low resale value compared to the domestic German brands. The C 110 also received negative points because of the undamped short swing arm on the front wheel.

A typical feature of the C 100 was the trapezoidal-oval speedometer, here by Yazaki, with the Honda Motors logo and four-digit counter display.

In addition to the moped version of the C 100, Honda also tried to sell a reduced-power 40 kph (24.8 mph) light motorcycle variant assembled at the Belgian branch in Aalst. But the CGM 100, like its moped counterpart, could not compete with the sporty two-stroke light motorcycles and was dropped from the sales program in 1965. In the US, on the other hand, 265,000 Americans opted for the 4.5 hp Super Cub in the same year.

THE "NEW" ENGINE PROVIDES EXTRA OOMPH

The weaknesses and flaws of the C 100 and C 110 models did not go unheeded in Japan. Extremely sharp driving could, in the long run, take its toll on the C 110 engine, which was lubricated with only centrifugal oil and also had just 0.6 liters (20.3 ounces) of oil in the sump. Honda put its money where its mouth was: as early as 1963, a new engine with an overhead camshaft was designed, and a genuine sports motorcycle, the CS 90, was developed. Naturally, the new bike received the four-speed transmission from the C 110. With a displacement of 89.5 cc, the engine delivered 7.5 hp in contrast to the 6.5 hp of the previous C 200 and the Scooterette model CM 90. Honda now no longer relied on centrifugal lubrication, so the new design received an oil pump, a strainer in the sump, and—last but not least—a centrifugal filter. Both the cylinder and cylinder head were now made of light metal, with the complete combustion chamber dome made of gray cast iron—valve seat inserts falling out or coming loose were thus not an issue with Honda's single-cylinder engines. The camshaft chain was always correctly tensioned by a small gear under spring pressure on the upper run of the timing chain.

The CS 50, first presented in 1964 at the Cologne IFMA, was the spitting image of its big sister, the CS 90. The moped with a telescopic fork and modern pressed-steel frame backbone was also available abroad as the CS 65. In that version, the oversquare engine revved at 10,000 rpm and delivered 6.2 hp to the rear wheel; in Germany, the fifties with their 39 mm bore managed "only" 5.2 hp. Of course, the dealer network of the Honda branch in Hamburg was nowhere near as finely meshed as those of its native German counterparts. With advertising ("Honda – the magic horse of our time") and price reductions (from 1,190 marks in 1967 to 995 marks in the spring of 1968), the importer tried to optimize its share of moped sales. But while Hercules, Kreidler, and Zündapp were haggling over tenths of a horsepower and Kreidler's RS officially loosened up to 6.25 hp from 1971 onward, the SS 50s were standing like lead. In 1976, the four-stroke moped was dropped from Honda's sales program, while demand for the ST 50/70 Dax and Z 50 Monkey fun bikes (which we have not included here for space reasons – a story about these fun machines is available separately) increased steadily.

For several years in the 1970s, vehicles for the markets in Belgium, the Netherlands, Luxembourg, and England had to be equipped with pedals. This was the only way sixteen-year-olds could legally drive this type of vehicle.

The SS 50 had a nominal output of just over 5 hp and was thus logically inferior to the two-stroke competition with 6.25 hp. On the other hand, the Honda was significantly cheaper and ran on regular gasoline.

The CL 90, easily upgraded to Enduro standard, was more popular in Japan and also in the US than its road-going counterpart, the S 90, which was also offered in Germany for a brief time.

C MODELS WITH OVERHEAD CAM ENGINES: UNSTOPPABLE

In 1966, the C 100 was replaced by the new C 50 overhead cam model. In Great Britain, the semiautomatic C 50 was available beginning in February 1967, and the C 90 was offered as a higher-displacement variant from September of the same year. Apart from their power units, the newer models differed from the OHV variants only in cosmetics: larger round turn signals, new steering heads with more plastic, and different round mufflers were fitted. An off-road variant, the CT 90, replaced the previous CT 200 models (*see picture*) for the US and Australia. The CT 90 was also available in a 50 cc version; all CT models had a dual-stage transmission, so the sheepherder in the outback and the recreational off-roader from Helsingør had a choice of six gears. For off-road riding, overseas customers could choose between the CL, which was nothing more than an S 90 with raised handlebars and raised exhaust, and the SL 90, which seemed better equipped for off-road driving thanks to more ground clearance, engine protection from below, and more suspension travel.

These vehicles are rare in central Europe, but the C models are still a common sight on the streets of Greece and England. Anyone walking through modern-day London, where cab license aspirants get to know the streets on their Cub 90 "knowledge bikes," or on the Greek islands will see that these little Hondas are still omnipresent—and this is even more true in all corners of Asia. This is true despite the market being flooded with an increasing number of "rolling cough drops" with variomatics and in a wide variety of displacements and designs. With just under thirty million units, these C 90 models have long since outstripped milestones achieved by vehicles such as the VW Beetle and Ford's Model T, now equipped with 12-volt electrics, a fuel gauge, and improved gearshift sequence. And anyone who thinks that the quality has somehow deteriorated is mistaken. In order to get into *The Guinness Book of Records*, at the end of the 1990s, Briton Adam Paul rode a C 90 from Cape Horn to the Cape of Good Hope—a little trip of 47,845 miles (77,000 kilometers)!

Everyone got along with the C 100—and everyone was nice: Grey Advertising's US ad campaign was everywhere, and the slogan was used for several years with huge success.

In the Netherlands, the SS 50's fuel tank could be personalized with "special paint." The Scooterette models also became more colorful in England and France as ZZ versions from 1975.

MY HONDA STORY

C CLASS FOR BEGINNERS

The C 50 appeared in England in the spring of 1967, not as a replacement for the Super Cub but as an update. Like so many others, Claire Leavey, an editor and graphic designer from England, began her riding experience on two wheels on the 50 cc Honda with the overhead-cam four-stroke. With 4.5 hp, the bike was still capable of over 70 kph (43.5 mph) at the end of the 1980s – which Leavey, then a schoolgirl, always pushed to the limit. Looking back, Leavey fondly recalls her adventures with her C 50.

Forty-five miles per hour, or over 70 kph, that's pretty fast when you're virtually squatting on a piece of paper. But with a little patience and in a crouched position, that was always possible on the derestricted C 50. After all, it was my first serious machine. And I emphasize "serious"!

There is a photo where, if you look closely, you can see a piece of paper that I taped to the leg plate, right next to the tax disc. It showed the exact route from my then pad in London's East End to my parents' house on the Welsh border. The picture reminds me of my very first return trip back then—one of many on the little Honda. Back then, you could still show up at the station with it in England and just put the Honda in the baggage car. My initial experiences the week before were pretty shaky—at least that's how I felt about the seemingly endless one-lane road system between Paddington Station and the distant East End. Other than the old *A–Z London Street Guide*, I had nothing to orient myself by. And some of the street layouts had been completely redesigned since the book had been printed—that was the first thing I found out.

The piece of garden in the picture probably has a different, somewhat special memory for my little sister—her first ride, standing on the foot pegs, taking our garden table broadside of the leg shield and maneuvering the whole thing through the hedge, right into the flower bed behind it. She must have been standing on the gearshift, turned the throttle briefly, and was so overwhelmed by the forward momentum of the barely doll-sized engine that she couldn't find the brake and instead ripped the throttle wide open. While standing up, she then started screaming and almost passed out from the acceleration as she flew through the branches.

Admittedly, with a little tailwind, the whole thing was even more exciting. On a windy day, my daily ride to school could even turn into work. Tailwinds could blow the Honda and me up to over 50 miles per hour—if I hid perfectly behind the handlebars and kept the A2 folder streamlined instead of having to lug a backpack full of books, as I so often did. With a headwind, it was sometimes faster—and less tiring—to walk. Gusts from the side were dangerous—once I was flung completely helplessly across the entire two lanes of traffic when a crosswind caught me broadside. The Honda drifted over to the edge where a hill began, which finally broke the wind further up, and I finally regained control with the handlebars. Fortunately, the road was completely empty at the time and I survived (again).

Probably my craziest moment on the Honda was when I pulled into a field where a flea market was being held—undoubtedly going much too fast. I steered the Honda vigorously to the right through a narrow gate driveway and almost at full throttle. The tires tried their hand at the dusty field soil but slid around on it almost like snails on rock, while I held on it and the tread dug into the ground. Front fork and shocks danced pogo, the springs relaxed like in a well-lubricated telescope, as we then plowed upward over a ridge. Like the legs of a mosquito, we flew majestically over a crevice in the ground that suddenly appeared; it led right through the middle of a fat, deep tractor track. Finally, we hit the ground again, coming down hard as I finally found the brakes, forcing myself to shout an apology over to the park attendant who came yipping after us. In the meantime, I've ridden fancier machines than the little C, but never again have I made such an impressive performance.

Beginning in 1967, the coffee-brown C 90 was available in England. The C 70 (in the background, on which Andrea is sipping her soda) came just a few years later.

Wheels of fortune: For many people in Belgium, the Netherlands, and England, the C 50 was the vehicle on which they took their first driving tests—and, thanks to the robustness of the design, usually returned home without injury.

HONDA CZ 100 — FORERUNNER OF THE MINIBIKE

It began as a toy. Forty-four years later, it found its way to Honda enthusiast Gilles Schumacher.

HONDA'S SMALLEST MOTORCYCLE WAS THE CZ 100. IT IS NOW A MUCH-SOUGHT-AFTER COLLECTOR'S ITEM AND THEREFORE HAS BEEN DIFFICULT TO FIND FOR DECADES.

Successful motorcycle caricatures: Whether on 10-, 8-, or initially even 5-inch wheels, these tiny Hondas made a name for themselves and quickly became favorites among youths, boat owners, and campers.

This CZ has a subframe under the seat in order to achieve a halfway-acceptable seat height.

MY HONDA STORY

Gilles Schumacher, a passionate devotee of old Honda mini motorcycles, shares the story of how an original Honda CZ 100 came into his life . . . and how he painstakingly restored it to (beyond) its former glory.

When my work colleague, who knew of my passion for old Hondas, rubbed an ad in a local newspaper under my nose one morning, I was amazed. Pictured was a child's motorcycle—dusty, spider-legged, but obviously a Honda judging by the shape of the tank. "What kind of bizarre thing is that, with no suspension and tiny lawnmower wheels?" he asked.

I suspected it but still could hardly believe it. . . . Almost at my front door, an original Honda CZ 100 with red tank was in danger of gathering dust and rusting away. The machine on offer was the only CZ 100 sold here in Luxembourg, dating from 1965, and despite the poor ad photo, I recognized it immediately: a neglected but complete Honda Monkey on its flat Dunlop tires. Run down, covered with chrome rust spots, with a foul-smelling rusty broth in the tank—that's how the CZ 100 had been sitting in a gloomy garage for more than fifteen years. But the Nippon Seiki speedometer in the headlight showed only an incredible 2,286 kilometers (1,420 miles).

"Are you a Honda collector? You really only want to put it in the living room, don't you? You're not going to ride it on the street!" the salesman, obviously not exactly motorcycle savvy, asked me incredulously. He went on to explain to me that this funny little "children's motorcycle" had belonged to his deceased cousin. Take it, I thought, and without haggling I was soon the happy second owner of this rare Honda. I was lucky, because a little later the seller was swamped with calls.

BACK ON THE ROAD—WITH NO RADICAL RESTORATION

I decided to minimize restoration work on the mini Honda to keep the well-preserved paint and chrome parts as original as possible. The first thing to do was to get some fresh air into the flat Dunlop tires—it was unimaginable that the "bonsai tires" actually still held tight even after forty-four years. Dunlop Japan had even immortalized the company founder Sir John Dunlop on a detailed, vulcanized medallion on the sides of the 5-inchers. The tiny tires were even then available only through Honda and can no longer be found today.

The petite headlight housing also incorporates the speedometer—with a prominent dial. The CZ is so small that the owner could easily tuck it under his arm.

The CZ's muffler was fitted exactly into the rear left corner of the frame and looks more like a tool compartment or oil tank.

COMPARED TO THE YOUNGER MEMBERS OF THE MONKEY FAMILY, THE CZ SEEMS MUCH MORE PLAYFUL AND AWKWARD. IT HAS NO SUSPENSION, AND THE ONE-PIECE HANDLEBAR IS STILL NOT PRACTICAL, WHILE THE FUEL TANK COMES FROM THE C 110 PARTS WAREHOUSE.

No matter how small or large the rider of the CZ is, he looks like a giant—and no more than the wheels and fork are visible of the vehicle.

THE WILD ANIMAL HIBERNATES IN THE LIVING ROOM

Carefully, I removed the dust and dirt from the red mini Honda. While doing so, I saw that the red paint had only a few small rust spots. With Swiss oil cleaner and Samurai wax, I helped restore the dwarf's shine in three weeks of meticulous manual labor. Then I disassembled the tank to remove aggressive gasoline resin and the red rust particles. A handful of nuts, bolts, and earplugs helped remove everything corroded from the small 6-liter tank in evening-long, noisy hours of twisting and turning. After I was finally satisfied with the now-sparkling clean interior, I decided to apply a transparent tank sealer. After all, I wanted to protect the metallic appearance of the tank true to the original for the next forty-four years.

Then came the crucial question: What was the condition of the small OHV engine? Should it, could it, still run after being idle for so long? Judging by the kick-starter, the C 100's engine with cast-steel cylinder head had not seized up and even still had a usable compression. Then for a few days I poured a mixture of rust solvent and engine oil through the spark plug hole to loosen the piston rings and the flash rust in the cylinder. While carefully unscrewing the plug, I noticed that the original NGK C7HSA—albeit with a badly pitted electrode—was still faithfully doing its job here. After an oil change and a precise valve clearance and ignition check, I flooded the small carburetor for the first time, turned the choke lever down, and kicked. Suddenly, the little 4.5-horsepower engine coughed out a cloud of blue smoke, and after a few minutes it bubbled away without gulping and, thanks to the large muffler, very quietly and evenly.

I was actually forewarned by the battle scars I found on the Honda CZ 100; a bent license plate and the abraded throttle grip rubber testified to disagreements between the first owner and the wild little Monkey. With its 55 kg and maximum power at 9,500 rpm, the miniature can quickly stretch the driver's arms to orangutan size—a little later I knew how: into first gear, using the gearshift lever . . . and, whoa, I had to fight with a rising front wheel. With galloping feet, I took off at breakneck speed. Then I went into second gear without the clutch and ha ha ha . . . the mini front wheel rose again and the Monkey hissed away with me, until we reached a fearsome 45 kph (28 mph). Don't pull the handlebars, nice slow turn into the first traffic circle, and—watch out—I immediately scraped the foot pegs on the asphalt. Two degrees of lean and a banana wobble in the chassis . . . but that actually felt fast! But . . . no worries, I survived the first ride, the Honda Monkey too. The following summer, I could hardly control the grin on my face during the first joint old-timer ride in Luxembourg . . . the CZ 100 Monkey had bitten me, and it got a warm and dry place of honor in the living room until the next season.

Gilles likes to take his Honda midget out for a spin, but because of the small wheel size, he always has to keep a close eye on where he's steering.

The name "Monkey" first appeared in French brochures.

Safe Fun
For Beginners
Or Experts
HONDA 50 MINI TRAIL
3.50-18 knobby tyres • Telescopic fork • Internal-expanding brakes front and rear • 50 cc OHC 4-stroke engi
ue Town or Country Playbike
unique fun riding the trails or skipping back and forth
campus. And you'll attract envious attention wherever
quality Honda playbike. It's sized somewhere
aller mini-bikes and a full-sized motorcycle, but with
red of big bike quality and reliability. Simple controls
it, including an automatic clutch and 3-speed
72cc OHC 4-stroke engine. Fold-down handlebars,
and rear brakes and suspension. Big wheels, engine
shield, bright lamps for safe riding.
Always wear a helmet and
observe all traffic rules
for safe riding fun.
• 5 bhp / 8,000 rpm • 72 cc OHC 4-stroke single engine • 70 kg (154 lb) weight
automatic clutch • 4.00-10 tyres • 1,515 × 660 × 1,050 mm (60 × 26 × 41 in) dimensions
ct to change without notice. • Specification certified by Transport Ministry of Japan.
HONDA
CT-70 TRAIL
HONDA
TRAIL70
HONDA
Z50J
HONDA
Dès 16 ans...
te bien en Chaly. Parce
aux couleurs jeunes et
ssant (72 cc), assez
uple, pour supporter à la
eurs de la jeunesse
du temps. Qu'il
r exemple, ou qu'il neige,
le moteur 4 temps du Chaly démarre
imperturbablement. Il est aussi facteur
d'économie (du super, pas de mélange), de
sécurité (frein moteur) et de propreté (sans
mélange, pas d'huile qui brûle dans les
cylindres, donc pas de risque de cambouis
sur votre pantalon). Alors, dès 16 ans, avec
une simple licence A1, on est heureu
rouler en Chaly. Facile à conduire
(embrayage automatique), il est aussi
confortable (bonne selle biplace, susp
télescopiques et hydrauliques, garde-
enveloppants). En fait, ce mini Honda
s'adresse à tous les jeunes. De tous â
HONDA
Chaly CF 70
Honda France - 20, rue Pierre-Curie - 93170 Bagnolet - Tél. 360.01.00
HONDA FRANCE préfère TOTAL

TYPES AND MODEL RANGES

A wealth of options: Honda's line continues to expand.

THE CZ AND Z MODELS WERE ALREADY PRESENT IN FRANCE AND ENGLAND IN THE MID-1960s. IN GERMANY, THE TEEN MAGAZINE *BRAVO* AND THE CHILDREN'S TELEVISION PROGRAM *HALLO FREUNDE* DID PRESENT HONDA'S TINY MOTORCYCLE, BUT RATHER CONSERVATIVELY AS A "PFIFFIKUS" (SMART COOKIE). THE BREAKTHROUGH IN GERMANY DEFINITELY CAME WITH THE ST 50 AND THE 70 DAX, FEATURING A SUCCESSFUL CONCEPT WITH TWO SEATS AND A SPORTIER CHARACTER.

Now rather outdated is the cartoon American Indian that adorned the tank emblem of the Germanized Honda Mini.

Unlike on the French version, the seat on the Pfiffikus sits directly on the frame, without any additional elevation.

HONDA

DR. THOMAS BECKER IS A DENTIST WITH A SOFT SPOT FOR FUNNY HONDA SINGLES. WE WERE QUITE STUNNED DURING OUR VISIT TO HIS HOME IN OFFENBACH, GERMANY. HE EVEN HAD A Z 50 J NEATLY TUCKED AWAY IN A CLOSET.

While the SS 50, which succeeded the C 110, had already made its debut in the fall of 1964, Honda began work on a prototype of a larger version of the Monkey minibike in 1968. The new version was also to be designed for two-person operation. A 70 cc engine was also installed to meet customer demands for more power for off-road riding and more speed over longer distances. To this end, the new 50 cc OHC engine was bored out from 39 to 47 mm—unlike the C 65 unit, which with a bore of 44 mm reached full power only at 10,000 rpm.

The first prototype was very similar to the first production series, which was launched in 1969. The only differences were a smaller headlight (the same as that used on the Z 50 A Minitrail version) and a small speedometer, initially round. The seat, which was clearly designed for a second passenger, had a kind of adapter to which the exhaust was attached. The holes in the heat shield were punched in a horizontal striped pattern. Directly on the front fork was the front mudguard (analogous to the US CT 70 variant). There were no side emblems—instead, two Honda logos pressed from aluminum were bolted directly onto the frame, between the front fork and seat. The Keihin round slide carburetor had a larger passage than the Monkey component, and the intake manifold had a 90-degree angle—unlike on the SS 50, where the air filter had to be hidden in the frame rather than sitting in a funny cylinder with chrome caps. The prototype also dispensed with a tachometer.

As on the Monkey Z 50, the two handlebar halves were fixed by hard rubber toggles in V-shaped recesses in the upper triple clamp—and they opened and folded down in an instant, so that the minibike could be easily stowed in the trunk of a vehicle or fit in the back seat. For export, the newcomer was given the nickname Dax (derived from "Dachshund").

The ST 70 got its name because of its elongated T-shape frame, the rear of which also concealed the small fuel tank—under the seat, like that of the Super Cub. The entire chassis thus looked quite similar to the physique of the dachshund dog breed. The ST 70 Z model was equipped with the usual foot-shifted three-speed transmission, the automatic centrifugal clutch, and a sporty camshaft. Two versions were available at once: the "classic" version and a sportier Type 2. Optionally painted in candy red, candy blue, and candy gold, the classic version had a short, bottom-exit exhaust that the CF 50/70 Chaly would later inherit—the emblems were mounted as on the prototype. Here, larger, ducktail-shaped mudguards were fitted, painted silver to add more expression to the classic image. Type 2 had smaller chrome fenders and a sporty high exhaust. Here the logos were stickers that had a sporty black-and-white-stripe pattern. This model was launched in candy red, candy blue, and a special candy yellow. In contrast to the prototype, both variants had a larger headlight and a triangular speedometer.

Monkey and Dax guru Walter Rein displays his golden-anniversary Z 50 (*top right*). In Japan, the Dax was reworked in the early 1990s as the AB 23. Its four-legged namesake can be seen on the seat in the advertisement below.

The Z 50 M was offered in the US without road registration, while the Dax was basically called the CT 70 and was always referred to as a "trail bike" in America.

Specifically for the US market, Honda built a second model in the same year; it was called the Trail CT 70 and based on the ST 70. This model was built mainly for the purpose of riding dirt roads and rougher terrain. The Trail CT 70 did not have folding handlebars, and the front mudguard was mounted directly on the front fork, so it sat higher than on the Japanese version. The CT 70 had a chrome mount that prevented too much dirt from collecting between the wheel and the mudguard. In addition, an engine guard called a "bash plate" sat beneath the CT 70's engine to prevent stone chips during off-road riding. The CT 70 K0 was launched on the market in 1969 in two versions: the CT 70 K0 standard version, with a three-speed semiautomatic transmission (in candy red, candy blue, and candy gold colors), and the CT 70 HK0, with a four-speed manual transmission that was hand-clutched (in candy orange, candy green, and candy blue-green colors).

At the same time, Honda also produced the Dax for the European market, which admittedly took some time, since each country in Europe had different legislation and registration regulations. In 1970, the first European Dax machines were sold and bore the name KI. Initially, the STs were sold in Europe in two versions. In addition to the ST 70—especially for the German market—there was a reduced-power 50 cc version called the ST 50 GE (General Export) starting in 1973. The ST 50 was thus sold as a "Mokick" with an insurance plate, and the ST 70 as a motorcycle (from the age of eighteen, it could be purchased only with the then Class 1 driver's license). This version was officially capable of just 40 kph (24.8 mph), and it had a flywheel as a throttle with centrifugal adjustment of the ignition, a smaller carburetor, and a cylinder head with a smaller intake, while retaining the standard camshaft.

Within the various countries, there were also all kinds of visual differences. For England and France, for example, there were larger, rectangular taillights, and the headlight and speedometer were also different. The German version was equipped with ducktail-shaped mudguards in conjunction with a high-mounted exhaust and a larger headlight and high beam including switchgear, combined with a square speedometer. Only the ST 70 variant had turn signals and high beams with switches in Germany. In Germany, mandatory minimum distances for turn signals required long stalks, and the chrome carrier was standard. The taillight was round, with an integrated orange brake light above.

Besides the usual ST 70, Honda also produced a special edition called "White Dax" or "Lady Dax." It was white with white, black, and green decals and had a seat that had a green floral pattern on top. This model—like the US CT 70 variant with manual clutch and four-speed transmission—is one of the most sought-after variants today and is rarely found in original condition.

In 1972, the ST 90 made a brief appearance on the market. It was the big brother of the Dax (with a stronger frame) and was therefore sometimes called the "Mighty Dax," which fit perfectly into the new US advertising strategy: "From Mighty to Mini. We have it all." Honda used the 90 cc engine in order to refine the CT 90 trail series, which sold magnificently for use in light terrain. Its 14-inch wheels earned the ST 90 the nickname "Fat Harry." Unfortunately, it was offered only in the US and was in the sales program there for only three years. In 1978, the K3 variant, a new design by Honda, came on to the market. The biggest differences from the previous models were the colors and the newly designed decoration. There were four versions: candy red with white-blue-black flame-shaped stripes, candy blue with yellow-black-white flames, green with yellow-black-white flames, and orange with yellow-black-white flames. That same year, Honda Germany stopped selling the ST 70.

In Great Britain, on the other hand, a version in candy brown with yellow, black, and white stripe decoration was also offered. The last ST 50 and ST 70 models for Europe were followed by the CY 50 (international designation: "Naughty Dax"), a different vehicle concept with an upright cylinder head, plastic mudguards, and thicker tires—which was intended to make the successor saltwater-safe and suitable for use on the beach. However, Honda continued to produce the CT 70 for the US. It was equipped with a hydraulic front fork (KI version) in 1972. In each model year, there were small changes: a single standing speedometer, different taillights, plastic fenders, different decoration, a black exhaust, and other heat shields. In 1973, Honda ended production of the CT 70 KII (H series), with manual clutch and four-speed transmission, but it continued to offer the three-speed semiautomatic variant of the CT 70.

DIFFERENT OFFERINGS FROM AALST

SMALL HONDA FOUR-STROKES WITH PEDALS

Like with the C 100 Super Cub, the paramount features of the "Little Hondas" that were produced between 1963 and 1976 at the first Honda plant in Aalst, Belgium, were economy and user-friendliness.

On April 21, 1968, it was drizzling in Wylye, a small English village in the county of Wiltshire. For Daniel Nash, this was no reason not to try out his latest acquisition: a bright red Honda P 50. The insurance premium had cost the retiree two British pounds, and he had to pay the same amount again for the small, round "Road Tax" sticker. At fifty-two pounds, four shillings, and nine pence, the funny moped with "Little Honda" written on it in large letters was much cheaper than the Honda C 50 owned by Daniel's neighbor Geoffrey Straw, who had to pay seventy-nine pounds and nineteen shillings for it at the same Honda dealer in Salisbury. But the P 50 was also much slower; a moderate 1.2 hp accelerated the 17-inch runabout to 25 mph, while Straw's Honda, which was also red, was capable of a top speed of almost 40 miles per hour.

Daniel had opted for the P 50 because the strange pressed-plate moped was considered foolproof. Geoffrey's C 50 was also light, but Daniel could not come to terms with the three-speed shifter mounted on the left. During a test ride, he almost crashed into the Anglican church. "Somehow I must have been thinking of my old Francis Barnett. It had its gearshift on the right," he explained as he apologized to the startled owner. Daniel had already filled the small tank of the P 50 with 2.5 liters (2/3 of a gallon) of 2-Star gasoline, and now he was ready to go. After a quick step on the pedals, he pulled the little lever on the left of the handlebars, then released it . . . and the OHC engine sprang to life.

Europe required special measures, and Honda took them to heart. The icebreakers were 50 cc machines.

After exploring various locations, the manufacturer built the first Honda plant on European soil in Aalst, Belgium.

Before the C 310 A with manual transmission was created from a rare C 240, C 100s were the first product to roll off the production line.

The P 50 was made precisely for customers like Mr. Nash. The Honda developers had gone to a lot of trouble with the 45-kilo (99-pound) lightweight. The concept of integrating the engine directly into the rear wheel had obviously been seen at Cyclemaster. In the 1950s this manufacturer from London had installed an auxiliary engine, which also had a hub engine in the rear wheel—and sold 100,000 of them within two years. But while the English produced a simple two-stroke engine, the P 50 (which was sold in Japan as the P 25) had a quiet four-stroke engine. Honda had already gained experience with the centrifugal clutch (well hidden here in the rear wheel hub, together with the triple chain gear and brake drum) on the C 100 Super Cub. The Keihin carburetor breathed filtered air, which was sucked into the cylinder under the single saddle. The chrome-plated manifold, which was routed around the rear wheel at the front and led into a round muffler on the other side, was also bizarre in appearance. A switch on the rear of the engine allowed the engine and rear wheel to be decoupled, so that the machine could also be used as a bicycle if necessary (for example, when the fuel tank was empty).

The "Little Honda" was manufactured in Japan from 1966 onward, and 24,892 examples of the "small" version with the typical 17-inch wheels were exported. However, the P 50 also rolled off the production line in Belgium. In 1962, the first Honda production facility outside Japan had been established in Aalst, and the P 50 was presented there in 1967, with this version being produced with 19-inch wheels. While the Japanese P 50 was available in scarlet (red), sky blue, and charcoal gray, all 1,128 units from Aalst were painted gray, sparing customers the agony of color choice.

Years earlier, Honda had already developed two other unusual mopeds at this location. The C 310, produced as the A and S versions, could pass at first glance for a four-stroke Zündapp Combinette with its egg-shaped tank and old-fashioned design. The 320 S, which was later offered in a modified form in the Netherlands as the TS 50, was the sports version with a knee-high tank. Common to all of them were the pedals, which were mandatory in Belgium and the Netherlands, and a three-speed twist-grip gearshift.Like the Cub engine, the C 310/320's engine was an OHV unit with a gear ratio of 3.562/2.041/1.4, but it was based on the C 240 Port Cub, a slimmed-down special variant of the C 100 that was built in Japan for only a full two years. As a moped, the Aalst version of the C 310 A was capable of 40 kph (24.8 mph). The high-torque engine, powered by a Keihin DPS 13NA or Mikuni MDZ 12 carburetor, produced 1.4 hp at 3,800 rpm.

The C 310 was adorned with a white plastic shield in Super Cub style, above which the small 4.5-liter tank was enthroned. In contrast, the C 320 was styled as a small motorcycle and was available only in black. In the mid-1960s, when the SS 50 was already being presented at the Frankfurt IFMA, another transitional model rolled off the production line in Belgium; the 310 S and its sportier counterpart, the C 320 S, received a new cylinder head with the hemispherical combustion chamber of the C 110 / C 114. The old C 310 models, of which a more powerful 2.2 hp version capable of 60 kph (37.3 mph) was also offered in the meantime, still had the ribbed cylinder head cover and parallel valves.

Novelty with wheel hub motor: the P 50 was presented to dealers at a major event in 1966. This variant with 19-inch wheels was produced for the Netherlands.

A leg shield was also available as an accessory for fully automatic PC 50s; the C 310 A had a manual three-speed transmission, pedals, and an OHV engine.

In Germany, Honda was still having a hard time in the "shot glass class." The Hamburg importer Meller had already failed to secure any significant market share for the Super Cub in the early 1960s, and European Honda Motor Trading GmbH also failed to achieve this success. Even full-page ads in the trade journal *Das Motorrad* were of no help, and *BRAVO* magazine readers certainly didn't seem to want to know anything about the small four-strokes from the Far East. The reason was obvious: while the CGM 100, restricted to 1.9 hp, could reach 40 kph (24.8 mph), the Super Cub proved to be a decidedly lame duck compared to the lively two-stroke competition.

Unfortunately, Daniel's favorite, the Honda P 50, which was offered in Germany starting in 1968 for 498 marks, met a similar fate. Honda had decided to reduce the output of the OHC engine to 0.8 hp at 3,500 rpm, and thus the Little Honda—which, according to the brochure, "whispered in four-four time"—never got going at all. "And those who started tuning often ran into problems with the valve train," recalls a longtime Honda dealer. In fact, the intake valve on the P 50 runs directly in the light-alloy cylinder head without a valve guide and often receives too little lubricant because of the centrifugal lubrication system with no oil pump, which in the worst case leads to valve breakage. Honda 50 connoisseur Carl Squirrell has prepared tailor-made solutions specifically for this problem child.

MOTO RETRO WIEZE PRESENTS
HONDA AALST:1963-2013
EXPO Madc by : HONDA CLASSIC BIKES CLUB BELGIUM
21 & 22 SEPT 2013
MOTO RETRO WIEZE
HONDA

ON THE FIFTIETH ANNIVERSARY OF THE FIRST EUROPEAN HONDA PLANT IN AALST, THERE WAS A SPECIAL EXHIBITION AT THE MOTO RETRO VINTAGE MOTORCYCLE SHOW IN WIEZE, BELGIUM, WITH ALL THE MODELS THAT HAD ROLLED OFF THE PRODUCTION LINE THERE, INCLUDING THE C 100.

For those who wanted it sportier: the PS 50 was a faster version of the PC 50, but it was reserved only for the Belgium/ Netherlands/Luxem-bourg market.

Why of all things the P 50 was christened "Little Honda" in German-language advertising material, no one knows.

Only the speedometers of the first series bore the nickname on the dial. For Germany, the official moped version was rated at 0.8 hp.

From April 1968, the P 50 was replaced in Great Britain by the first version of the PC 50; in the Netherlands, both models were sold in parallel and even supplemented by a sportier version in 1969: the PS 50, which resulted in the reappearance of a three-speed *bromfiets* (moped). Sold as the "Little Honda PS 50," the 40 kph (24.8 mph) moped initially had a 5.5-liter tank; later versions received a 7-liter tank. The most interesting version was undoubtedly the filigree PS 50 L (L for luxury) in bright yellow with chrome tank and double seat. In 1970, the basic version of the P 50, with the engine in the rear wheel, cost 469 guilders; the PS 50, starting at 649 guilders, was already considerably more expensive at that time. In the same year, the PF 50 Amigo was presented in Aalst, again with single-speed gearing and automatic clutch. Another version, also with a tubular frame instead of the previously used pressed-sheet-metal frame and styling comparable to Kreidler or Hercules mopeds, was called the PF 50 DXR, with the nickname Novio, and was also offered in England. Common to all engines was the cylinder inclined upward by 10 degrees. From 1970, all engines were again equipped with a bottom-mounted cam-shaft and trochoidal oil pump, and power had increased to 1.8 hp at 5,750 rpm. The PF 50 weighed 48.5 kilograms (107 pounds) empty, while the PC 50 weighed exactly 50 kilograms (about 110 pounds). The engine with 42 mm bore and 35.6 mm stroke was still based on the first P 50 engine. In 1970, Honda "Holland" replaced the elaborate C 310 and C 320 with a C 50 H converted to pedals. In contrast, the PC 50 remained in the program at Honda UK until 1976.

Whether the P 50, PC, PS, PF, or C 310/320 — all pedal four-strokes are now classics. Halfway-decent PC 50s have long been rare in England and can rarely be found for less than a thousand euros. Even in the Netherlands, they are rare and can rarely be found for less than eight hundred euros; even examples in poor shape sell for four hundred euros. C 310s are somewhat more expensive, and the C 320 / TS 50 already reaches the Honda SS 50 level. Important with all mopeds is that the oil must be changed regularly. By the way, there is no reason to buy expensive spare parts lists and operating manuals at internet auctions, because these documents are available at www.hondaheaven.org for free. Information on the Honda P 50 can be found on the internet by using the search terms "Carl Squirrell" and "Honda P50."

A youthful dream with pedals: The sporty C 320 is shown here with a modified cylinder head, which was also installed on the C 310 S. This Honda is probably the most sought-after 50 made in Aalst, Belgium.

MY HONDA STORY

Only a handful of P 50s found buyers in Germany. As on the PC and PS 50, a lever could be used to disengage the engine if the rider runs out of fuel.

1967 HONDA P 50

The German Honda importer also wanted to get involved in the moped class in the 1960s. Unusual but of high technical quality, the first moped from Japan remained exotic in Germany—and something of a wallflower.

Uncle Ludwig is beaming in the Lower Bavarian July sun. His neighbor, a pretty girl who had recently moved in, has just rung his doorbell in despair because her old Golf has unexpectedly gone on strike—on her first day of work! Should she take the bus?

"Well, I've got something better," Ludwig explains to her. "I've got a moped. It's bright red, and I can even use it as a bicycle when I forget to take it to the gas station."

Gulp! The businesswoman says she hasn't ridden such a rattletrap since her schooldays, but Ludwig reassures her, "All you have to do is give it gas and use the brakes."

Five minutes later the thing is ready to start, and helpful Ludwig offers a few instructions. First, open the fuel valve behind the seat, then pull the lever with the C on the steering head a little upward. Then it's time for a few brisk pedal strokes and then to pull the small deco lever on the left, release it, and immediately turn the throttle grip inward. A quiet chug sounds next to the rear wheel, and the red two-wheeler accelerates its rider to the permitted 25 kph (15.5 mph), as indicated by the Denso speedometer in the lamp housing. A few braking tests later, the newly qualified Honda rider even has the confidence to ride one-handed, because as a four-stroke, the single cylinder integrated in the rear wheel also brakes by itself somewhat when the throttle is released. When she takes the last bend and sees the rest of the rolling gravel, she luckily remembers the last tip from her neighbor: first brake the rear wheel so that the front wheel doesn't suddenly understeer.

But now she has to go or she'll miss her first meeting. But Ludwig, in his lederhosen, still wants to explain to her where she can find the next gas station and, above all, where the release lever is located, in case the engine simply doesn't want to go and the red Honda has to function as a bicycle. She's amazed at how simple it is: simply flip the inconspicuous lever on the engine and pedal instead of using the throttle. The lady's handbag is quickly tied on securely, the deco lever clicks back into its original position, and she whirs away in her skirt and sunglasses.

"My, was that thing always so fast?" wonders Ludwig and waves.

"LITTLE HONDA": P FOR PEDAL POWER

Soichiro Honda wanted to round off the Honda two-wheeler range with a flyweight for the ladies—or to put it another way, a rolling shopping basket. The "Little Honda," as it was officially called, was therefore to feature a low step-through like the successful Super Cub model. It was decided to revisit the hub-engine concept with which Honda had started after World War II. The vehicle was to be so light that—like the French VéloSolex—it could also be comfortably used as a bicycle.

Although the basic features of the 12 kg lightweight engine, such as the cylinder raised 10 degrees from the horizontal, were based on the Super Cub unit, on closer inspection it was a completely independent engine with an overhead camshaft and valves working in parallel, both with 15 mm head discs. The bore and stroke of the short-stroke engine were 42 × 35.6 mm. Unlike the newly revised Super Cub unit, which now had an oil pump installed, the hub motor still operated with centrifugal lubrication, and instead of relying on a battery, a magneto igniter provided the necessary spark. Power was transmitted to the rear wheel (invisible from the outside because it was encapsulated) via a centrifugal clutch and a total of three chains with associated sprocket pairs. The pressed-steel frame's steering head contained a short swing arm, and the rear wheel and drive were not sprung for cost reasons. To ensure legroom, the engineers placed the 2.5-liter fuel tank above the rear wheel. However, this blocked the usual luggage space, so as an alternative, a luggage rack was positioned above the front wheel, and a basket could be fitted as an accessory. In contrast to the simple 90 mm drum brake on the front wheel, the rear wheel hub housed a somewhat larger external shoe brake, whose mode of operation was somewhat unusual. Interestingly, the P 50 was manufactured not only in Japan but also in the first European Honda factory, which was built in Aalst, Belgium, in 1962. The versions differed not only in color but also in wheel size. The Japanese variant, delivered in red, sky blue, or gray, rolled on 17-inch wheels, while the "Little Honda" assembled in Belgium was sold exclusively in gray and featured 19-inch wheels.

The P 50 began rolling off the production line in June 1966 and was available at Honda dealers in the UK starting in December. There, and in Belgium, the Netherlands, and Luxembourg, the Honda became a bestseller. Over 25,000 units were registered in the next two years in the United Kingdom alone, where Honda had long been a big player in the entry-level sector thanks to the Super Cub. With a purchase price of fifty-two pounds, four shillings, and nine pence, it was even significantly cheaper on the island than the Super Cub's successor, the Honda C 50 (seventy-nine pounds and nineteen shillings). In the Netherlands, the first Honda "Bromfiets" was available for 469 guilders and was even offered in parallel with its conventional successor, the PC 50, in 1969.

European Honda Motor Trading GmbH, by then based at Wandalenweg 4 in Hamburg, Germany, had the 45 kg lightweight in its range starting in 1967. However, the high-revving four-stroke's output had to be reduced from 1.38 to less than 1 hp, because it did not fit into the prescribed scheme and exceeded the moped limit in terms of speed (25 kph [15.5 mph]) and rated rpm (4,800 rpm). This change was a mistake. With changed ignition timing and a new carburetor assembly, the German P 50 was quiet as a whisper, as the German advertisement promised, but still ran at 3,500 rpm, while the centrifugal clutch's frictional connection occurred at just under 3,000 revs. Honda dealers were still thin on the ground—unlike those of the service networks of Hercules, the Zweirad Union, or Zündapp, for example. Only about thirty examples of the "Little Honda" are said to have been sold in Germany. It was not mentioned in the press until the late fall of 1968, when it was featured in a short test in *Motorrad* under the title "Gifts." Richard Traub praised the moped's simple operation, and to him it was "the sensation." And he explained, even if it probably doesn't impress anyone much, "The Honda P 50 is the only moped with a four-stroke engine among all the two-stroke competition." While that was commendable, it came too late, because the production of this unique vehicle was halted in April 1968.

HERCULES

Moped & Mokick-Programm 73

COMPETITION REVS UP

Successfully copying winning concepts—Honda's competitors try their best but have mixed results.

OF COURSE, THE SUPER CUB'S SUCCESS DID NOT REMAIN A SECRET FOR LONG. WHEN IT CAME TO NEW MEMBERS OF THE LEGION OF SMALL MOTORCYCLES, THE QUESTION OF WHETHER THE CHICKEN OR THE EGG CAME FIRST CANNOT BE ANSWERED. IN THE US, FOR EXAMPLE, MINIBIKES SPROUTED LIKE MUSHROOMS IN THE 1960s.

Yamaha developed its own "Scooterette" with a two-stroke engine in the 1960s (*left*). With a liquid-cooled engine and Solomatik, the 40 kph version from the manufacturer Solo, based in Sindelfingen, Germany, had 2.2 hp (*right*).

The RV 50 from Suzuki seemed more grown up than the ST 50/70. It was also produced as RV 90 and RV 12.

Suzuki developed fierce competitors for the Asian market, which boasted perfectly metered separate lubrication, fan cooling, their own semiautomatic transmission, and a telescopic fork. *Below*: Japanese teens could choose between the Honda MB 50 and the CB 50.

When the Super Cub was introduced, the Colleda models had already been successfully rolling off the production line at Suzuki for years. This was despite the fact that Michio Suzuki's company had actually started out with completely different intentions and materials—the processing of silk—and had begun building motorcycles only in 1954. As early as 1958, Suzuki technicians put their first vehicle, the Suzumoped, on wheels. The drive was provided by a previously manufactured auxiliary engine, which was visually inspired by the German NSU Quickly. Soon thereafter, the first representative of the large-wheel scooters with two-stroke engines appeared there. It was called the Selpet, and its fuel tank was still in the front in the foot well, like the motorcycle model. The technicians at Suzuki paid particular attention to details, so the MA 50 had an electric starter, turn signals, and a four-speed gearbox. With a dry weight of 130 pounds (58 kg), the little Suzuki easily managed 37 mph (60 kph). It was not until 1963 that a successor model, the M 30 Selpet, arrived on the market, with the tank also placed under the seat, thus completely implementing the concept of the C 100. With its 3.5-liter (0.9 gallon) tank, the M 30 was supposed to have a range of 223 miles and—according to official manufacturer data—be capable of 43.5 mph (70 kph).

The M 30 did not come to England until 1966, and a 55 cc counterpart called the M 31 Suzy was also sold in Japan. These semiautomatic Suzukis were still technically designed for mixture lubrication—and thus were not even on a par with the Super Cub. In the spring of 1968, however, a new variant was introduced in England: the U 50, which had a separate oil tank with a pump for mixing in the lubricant. Between 1971 and 1974, the better-equipped F 50 was able to hold its own against Honda's C models as well as could be expected. In 1974 came the FR 50, followed by the FR 70 from 1975. An improved FR 80 was to stand up to the Honda C 90 starting in late summer of 1976—and beginning in 1980, a likewise redesigned FS 50 began its sales career.

Offered in Japan and France as the VanVan 50, the cuddly Suzuki was a serious competitor to the small motorcycles from Honda. In addition to the CY 50, the CB 50 was also added to the Honda program as a Dax replacement.

With just under 7 hp at 5,500 rpm, the FR 80 was a match for the Honda, because thanks to its powerful two-stroke engine with diaphragm intake control, it could also sometimes pull away in third gear if the traffic light situation or driver negligence required it. In terms of acceleration, the FR 80 was definitely superior to the Honda 90, but above 31 mph (50 kph), noise and vibration were annoying at times. The brakes also reliably slowed down the FR—known on the island as the "Scooterette"—even though the short swing arm tended to sway more than that of its four-stroke competitor.

The ideas of Yamaha from Hamamatsu were not entirely different, but idiosyncratic. The company was founded as Yamaha Nippon Gakki Seizō Kabushiki Kaisha (Nippon Gakki Company Limited) in 1887 by Torakusu Yamaha—as a maker of pianos. Just 125 YA-1 Akatombo (Red Dragonfly) motorcycles were built as replicas of the German DKW RT125. The enormous demand for the improved YA-1 in 1955 led to the founding of Yamaha Motor Co. Ltd. The short-lived MF 1 was also offered in the US from 1958 as a 3.5 hp scooter on 16-inch wheels, but it was not until the start of the 1963 that advertisements appeared for the MJ 2, which was serious competition for Honda. Like the Honda C 102, Yamaha's beautifully designed family vehicle had an electric starter and was powered by a new two-stroke engine controlled by a diaphragm intake. Like the C 100/105, the 55 cc engine delivered its 5 hp to the rear wheel via a three-speed gearbox and fully enclosed chain. Incidentally, Yamaha also introduced its Autolube lubrication system in the same year. It was not until July 1965 that the new Autolube-equipped U 5 and U 5D Mate—sold in the US as the Newport 50—were launched, and they were joined by the 73 cc U 7 Mate variant in December 1965. As with Suzuki, a generational change took place in the early 1970s, with the V 50 and its higher-displacement V 90 variant. Yamaha had also long since caught up with the competition in terms of electrics. While Suzuki still used contact ignition in its engines, Hamamatsu relied on a modern transistor ignition. The Yamaha V 90 Mate had 12-volt electronics and a seat that was 26 inches (66 cm) long, but it was without an electric starter. It could reach just under 56 mph (90 kph) and impressed with unusual features such as an oil-level lamp, until 1985, when its successor, the Townmate, got down to business in a completely different way.

The maintenance-free cardan, together with a four-speed semiautomatic, has made the Townmate popular in England and Greece to the present day.

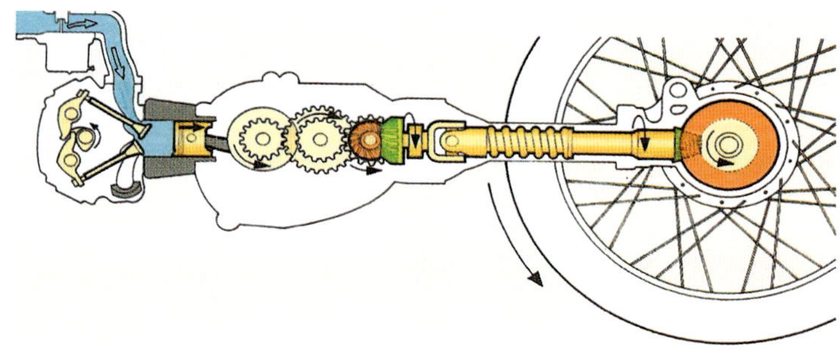

The T 80 Townmate was launched in 1984 with the chassis of the V 80 and a new four-stroke engine.

DOING THINGS DIFFERENTLY

Only the absence of oil revealed that the Townmate somehow got down to business differently than its predecessor. Instead of a two-stroke engine that was chain driven, this model had a four-stroke engine, four-speed gearbox with similar clutch (no lever necessary), and shaft drive. It is interesting to note, however, that even in the T 80 brochure from the last year of sale, "Autolube" could still be read under the heading "Lubrication," and "oil tank capacity" was actually still stated as 1 liter. Here the advertising department had clearly been asleep. But the truth was that twenty years after the Japanese two-stroke specialist Yamaha—despite Honda's budding supremacy—had powerfully stirred up the domestic motorcycle market with the Autolube grease system, it wanted to revive the market segment in certain European markets and stand up to their big competitor. The potential of the Scooterettes with their low step-through, centrifugal clutch, and low-maintenance drives had already been explored by the company's marketing people in the mid-1960s.

BORROWED TECHNOLOGY, SKILLFULLY USED

Initially intended for domestic customers, but also for the export market, another unusual city hopper concept was still being developed at the end of the 1970s, marketed as the QT 50. The minimalist-looking vehicle, nicknamed the Yamahopper, had single-speed gearing, an automatic clutch engine, footrests, and—unlike its competitors—a maintenance-free cardan drive. The tiny city vehicle rolled on 14-inch spoked rims until 1992, when the Cutie was produced and its drivetrain was also fitted to the Yamaha PW 50, a mini motorcycle for youngsters that was popular in Europe.

Paired with a horizontal OHC four-stroke that delivered its 6.5 hp to the rear wheel with four-speed shifting and a centrifugal clutch, the new Townmate got off to a good start, which was further underscored by its 495-pound price tag in England. Mat Oxley, then a freshly minted editor at *Motor Cycle Weekly*,

The US market followed its own rules, with minibikes made in the US selling very well there, as did Italian imports. The Yamaha Chappy was compact, light, and easy to ride, which also made it attractive in France.

was allowed to write about the first test in late summer 1983. An average fuel consumption of 2.5 liters per 100 km (94 mpg) was measured (best value: 2.06 liters [114 mpg]). "The thing easily maintains 80 kph (49.7 mph) and went through the light barrier at just under 92 kph (57 mph) on the MIRA test track, making the Yamaha faster than the C 90," Oxley wrote. However, the tester made no secret of his major criticisms: "Lousy suspension and the turn signal switch is on the wrong side" was his verdict, which was unfortunately just as true for the Honda C 90 ZZ.

In May 1986, the Townmate T 80 received a 50 cc counterpart, and both variants were also offered on the Greek market. Instead of the four-speed transmission, the T 50 had only three speeds, which were lower-geared overall. While the clutch was the same in dimension and number of discs, the centrifugal clutch on the "shot glass version" engaged much later (from 2,600 rpm, the T 80 from 2,100 rpm). While the development team had taken some trouble with the design and tuning of the engine, the chassis of the V 80 was only minimally modified. The engine was mounted in almost the same position as its two-stroke predecessor, and the fuel tank was only slightly modified, its capacity reduced by 0.3 liters. Due to the maintenance-free shaft drive, the wheelbase was moved back by 10 mm (0.4 inches), while the seat height increased due to the slightly higher upholstered seat from 730 to 750 mm (28.75 to 29.5 inches). The rotary fuel tank cap, which is held in position by a strut, closes perfectly—as does the ignition lock cover below the speedometer, which (as *Motor Cycle Weekly* noted thirty-six years ago) is amazingly accurate. The brake and short swing arm on this '87 version should be treated with caution, despite good lubrication and adjustment. Here, changes during a model update—more than a flat-chested 80 cc, for example—would certainly have yielded significant advantages. At the time, Oxley described the five-way preload-adjustable shock absorbers, even in new condition, as "barely up to the job," a damning judgment, which was true in fully loaded condition. Yamaha's cheap urban bike counterpart with cardan shaft was built until 1995 and sold until 1997. The Crypton, which was offered in Greece as a follow-on, was much sportier, but it was still equipped with chain drive. Admittedly, like the Innova and the Wave, it lacked that simple charm of minimalism.

Originally from Mansfield, Ohio, manufacturer Rupp found success among US youths with the Roadster 2. Trimmed for off-road use, the 4 hp machine had torque converters and 12-inch wheels.

MINIBIKE FEVER FOR MAXIMUM FUN

The Honda Z may have its origins in the Tama Tech amusement park, but the trend toward the minibike actually came from the US. It was founded by people such as Mickey Rupp, who started in the late 1950s in Ohio—with go-karts. In 1962, after initial sales successes, minibikes were put on wheels—initially 4- and 5-inch wheels, which soon gave way to 8- and 10-inchers. Early models such as the Dart had neither lights nor registration, and starting in 1971 they had automatic transmissions with torque converters and engines with fan cooling. Instead of Lauson engines, power units from the US compressor manufacturer Tecumseh were installed in 1968, and disc brakes were also fitted in the same year. The Roadster, Scrambler, Hustler, and Chopper models were extremely popular. The top seller from 1971 was the Black Widow, with a Tecumseh HS 40 engine with a Dellorto carburetor. The black minibike had chrome fenders and was marketed as a best-in-class off-road racing machine. Rupp Manufacturing became Rupp Industries in 1971. It had four hundred employees at the time and a development department of twenty-three people, with sales in the millions. In 1973, the company ran into financial difficulties, and the last Roadster models with 24-spoke wheels were sold in 1976.

Just how popular the smallest fun machines were in the US was shown by the fact that Harley-Davidson, then the owner of the Italian motorcycle manufacturer Aermacchi as AMF, was able to offer US customers a two-stroke minibike thanks to the Europeans. As early as 1960, Harley-Davidson had acquired 50 percent of Aermacchi's shares, and it then completely appropriated the company in 1974. Beginning in 1972, the Harley-Davidson MC-65 Shortster was available. Visually, it was a far more balanced vehicle than those of the competitors from Fox and Rupp. Dubbed "Shortster" by the marketing department to resemble the name of the 1,000 cc Sportster, the little newcomer had a central tube frame and proper oil-damped suspension elements. In addition, it was street legal with instruments and a braced handlebar. In accordance with the trend, it had an upswept exhaust compared to the Italian Leggero with a chrome cover. It also came with a dual seat and polished stainless-steel mudguards. Paint options were yellow, red, and blue. The wheelbase was 40 inches (1,016 mm), the wheels 3.00 × 10. In 1973, a 90 cc engine with four-speed gearbox was installed in the slightly modified frame, and the vehicle was renamed X 90. About 8,000 examples of the Shortster were produced.

Italian bikes—whether mini or maxi—were all the rage in the US in the 1960s and '70s. So was Benelli; Penney's Auto Center had three two-stroke minibikes with the characteristic triangular tank from Italy in its program. The smallest full automatic was christened Fuzzer and offered for $219. Those who added $80 could pick up the Dynamo Compact with four-speed gearbox, or available for $319 was the Scrambler variant with folding handlebars, knobby tires, and extra gearing.

Even the renowned manufacturer Harley-Davidson from Milwaukee got in on the minibike action, but the X 90 was a badge-engineered product from Italy.

Shortster... the mini-cycle that's mighty like a motorcycle.

Shortster's the little guy in the Harley-Davidson family. But its resemblance to our big machines tells you where it comes from . . . and where it belongs. It has mini-motocross forks up front and hydraulic shocks back aft to give you a backwoods ride like no other mini-bike you ever rode. A tough, 65cc two-stroke engine cranks out a bag of stump pullin' power. And puts it all on the ground through a three-speed foot shift. Shortster has full-sized levers and grips . . . just like the big guys. And a wide, comfortable seat that lets you hang in there all day long.

Cut loose and head for the good country. With Harley-Davidson's neat new Shortster . . . the mini-cycle that's mighty like a motorcycle. See for yourself. At your Harley-Davidson dealer. AMF | Harley-Davidson, Milwaukee, Wis.

Shortster, another outperformer from Harley-Davidson.

ROD & Custom

1320 HAULER

MORE! TWO-STROKE TUNING

PAINTING HOW-TO

HOT RODDERS GUIDE TO

In addition to the RV 90, Suzuki surprised the new generation in 1972 with the rotary-valve-intake-controlled MT 50 Trailhopper. The 3 hp machine was light, inexpensive, and capable of over 31 mph (50 kph).

As early as 1969, Leopoldo Tartarini surprised everyone with his Kit Kat minibike. The Giromat engine with automatic clutch was supplied by Franco Morini.

IN EUROPE: SMALL ITALIANS, GERMAN FREELOADERS, AND INTERESTING JAPANESE

Italjet boss and company founder Leopoldo Tartarini always had a special knack for special market niches. The son of Italian racer Egisto Tartarini, he not only was successful in long-distance motorcycle racing but also built MZ engines into his own chassis from 1957 onward in his company Italemmezeta, and later also Jawa, Triumph, and Yamaha engines. The Go-Go 50 was created in 1967 as a minibike to take home from San Lazzaro di Savena, and the first children's motorcycle was launched a year later as the Mini-Bambino. Things went even smaller and more imaginative with the Kit Kat 50, the first foldable moped. Not only in Europe but also in the US, the 2.2 hp motorcycle was a perfect alternative for vacationers. According to *Popular Science*, the Kit-Kat cost $315 at the dealership in Burbank, California. Folded up, the little Italian was just 43.3 × 20.5 × 19.7 inches (110 × 52 × 50 cm). The handlebars were foldable, and the saddle could also be lowered, so that the moped could easily be stored in the trunk of a car, in a motor home, or on a boat. The legendary 5-inch minibike was later developed into the Pack / Pack 2 moped, which was even exhibited in the Museum of Modern Art in New York. The Gyromat engine was designed by Franco Morini.

The introduction of the Dax, as I was told by Wolfgang Murrmann, who at that time was a member of the Honda Germany management, took place for authorized dealers at the same time as it was launched in the product range of the Hertie, Kaufhof, Horten, and Karstadt department store chains. The conditions were the same for reasons of competition. At that time, the magazine *Motorrad* also took pity and finally published in 1974 and 1975 multipage market overviews for the popular genre of small mopeds, mopeds, and mokicks—which admittedly reflected only part of what was on offer. The Honda ST 50 was called G 2, meaning GE = "general export." The list also included the Suzuki RV 50, then still imported under Fritz Röth. Soon the larger-displacement RV 90 and RV 125 VanVan were also available in Germany, of which Suzuki actually brought a new edition with a four-stroke engine onto the market a few years ago.

With fully automatic minis—the Yamaha LB 50 and 80 Chappy as well as the Bop—the Japanese motorcycle manufacturer Yamaha wanted to mix up the market in 1976. While a 1FO version of the Chappy was quite successful in Germany, and as the LB 80, with a 72 cc engine, easily reached 43.5 mph (70 kph), the Bop LB 3, also offered in 50 and 72 cc versions, was little in demand—and is therefore undoubtedly a rarity today.

From a technical point of view, however, Yamaha had leaned far out of the window: the two gears are conveniently shifted automatically. The engine contains two centrifugal clutches with different ratios, and the two-speed gearbox works by

The Pack 2 stands out as a cute descendant of the Kit Kat in New York's Museum of Modern Art. The Chappy with two-speed automatic was also successful in Japan. The Zippy, on the other hand, was more of a trendy gimmick, but it impressed with its fat 5.00-8-inch rear wheel.

linear actuator. While one centrifugal clutch is responsible for idling and starting, the second takes over shifting to the next gear. The engine has a lower range for steep hill climbs, which is activated by an additional lever on the engine. The small 49 cc two-stroke produces 2.8 hp at 5,000 rpm—perfect for the light 157-pound (71 kg), 8-inch runabout, which in Germany was available from Yamaha dealers for eight years: in 1976 for 1,482 marks, and then in 1984 for almost 2,400 marks. Unfortunately, the LB 50 IC Zippy was available only in Japan. Like the Chappy, it was also on 8-inch wheels, but it had a wild mix of wide rear wheel and narrow front wheel.

Two German minibikes were also in the mix at the time. Starting in 1972, the Nuremberg-based Hercules-Werke offered its sport bike as a moped with a five-speed gearbox or as a 24.8 mph (40 kph) throttle variant with a Sachs three-speed engine. At just under 49.7 mph (80 kph), the "big" SB variant certainly ran faster than the ST 70 from the factory, but it was expensive as far as insurance was concerned. Both variants were offered until 1979, but by as early as 1976 the little Franconian cost around 650 marks more than the Dax, with the Suzuki RV 50 right in the middle of the field. The bikes available from the Sindelfingen manufacturer Solo were likewise technologically conservative but paired with interesting design. The Solo 725 and the Solo 726 were called scooters by the Swabians. The 2.4 hp moped version had a two-speed automatic and was quite zippy—and durable, thanks to its sophisticated liquid cooling system for the two-stroke engine.

Honda
Trail Bikes

CLEVERLY AUGMENTED

When reaching the end of the road doesn't matter: an idea from the Americans, properly implemented, goes through the roof.

AN UNEXPECTED BOOST: IN THE US, OFF-ROAD METAMORPHOSES HELPED THE HONDA C 100 AND C 110 VARIANTS GREATLY.

Less is sometimes more. With the right gearing, the Super Cub mutated into a tractor par excellence, even off-road.

Little by little, the modified Super Cub acquired more horsepower and features that gave it tremendous advantages off-road.

MY HONDA STORY

THEY WERE AVAILABLE NOT ONLY AS CT MODELS, BUT ALSO AS SPORTIER CL OR SL VERSIONS. THIS ALSO PAVED THE WAY FOR THE 10-INCH ST 50 AND 70 MINI TRAIL MODELS. EVEN UNUSUAL COMBINATIONS SUCH AS THE QA 50 FOR THE SMALLEST RIDERS WERE POSSIBLE.

FOR HUNTERS AND COLLECTORS

In the 1960s, many motorcycle manufacturers came up with the idea of making their entry-level models into trendy off-road machines. The transformation of the Super Cub into an off-road bike for everyone took a long time, but the Trail Cub was more than just a catalyst for Honda's bestseller.

There is a bang and smoke; Ted curses. The bullet from the Weatherby Mark 5 has missed the big whitetail by a hair's breadth. "Well, let's call it a day," he thinks, and the passionate hunter kicks the kick-starter, slightly annoyed, after again stowing his rifle in the handlebar mount. He was luckier last week, especially since the beast weighed in at well over 150 pounds, as it turned out later at home in St. Louis.

The yellow Honda 90 makes its way through the swampy Missouri Ozarks, its rider easing off the throttle and pushing the shift lever into second gear with the ball of his foot. The $330 he spent on it was not a bad investment; even with the heavy load on the last hunting trip with Sam, the little Honda with its 6.5 hp engine didn't flag. It was Sam who had persuaded him to stop by the Honda dealer and take this funny thing out for a test ride. "The Honda Super Cub, that's only for women. You can't go off-road with it, let alone take a rifle or a deer piggyback," Ted had sneered at the time. Sam just said he should remember how thoroughly horribly the off-road attempt with the rickety Schwinn bike or the Indian Scout had gone. That they got the old 750 back on the road at all was a miracle. But the little Honda, on which Ted had just bumped back to his truck, was a real mountain goat on wheels—light, uncomplicated, and unbreakable, no matter whether it flew into the mud or whether the engine cheered at maximum speed in first gear.

While it may seem provocative now, in 1964, when the CT 200 was launched, an advertisement depicting a rifle at the ready was still regarded as politically correct. The ad clearly defines the 90 cc Honda's area of use: where the wild animals lived.

Remember her sister? The Honda Trail 55? This kid's the Trail 90 and she packs 30% more oomph.

Load her with 450 lbs. She'll make out better over rough terrain than anyone in the business.

The big push comes from the OHV single cylinder 4-stroke engine. She'll climb all over a 50% incline—if you feel so inclined. And deliver 160 mpg.

The Trail 90 comes with an automatic clutch, extra hand brake and the only standard-equipment spark arrestor approved by the USDA Forest Service.

If you like the athletic type, try the new Honda Trail 90. Price? $330 plus a modest set-up charge.

For address of your nearest dealer or other information, write: American Honda Motor Co., Inc., Dept. DH, 100 West Alondra, Gardena, California.

HONDA

world's biggest seller!

 9

Bag the game and go home. The Trail 55 already had a "bash plate," a guard under the engine. The rifle mount seen here is still a makeshift one.

The most important (hunting) features of the 55: sufficient space between front wheel and engine, a short off-road gear ratio, and the second brake lever on the handlebar—just in case.

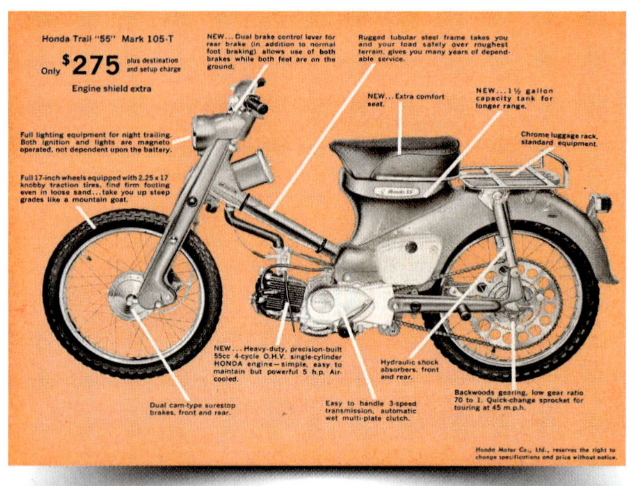

The little hoppers from Japan had appeared on the streets of America only a few years earlier. On July 4, 1959, Honda opened its first branch in California, a modest office and salesroom on Pico Boulevard in Los Angeles. Soichiro Honda's friend and right-hand man, Takeo Fujisawa, had decided to offer Honda's product line in the US, in keeping with Frank Sinatra's philosophy: "If you can make it there, you'll make it anywhere." Six Honda models were in the bag for Kihachiro Kawashima, who had been on the Super Cub development team and was appointed to the board of the newly formed American Honda Motor Company. He and his seven employees initially seemed to be at a loss in Los Angeles. Americans were skeptical; building a dealer network seemed an impossibility. "Our first year ended with a $54,000 loss, even though we had sold 1,732 motorcycles," Kawashima recalls.

"Honda was hoping for increasing demand for the 250 and 305 Dream in particular," he explained. On these higher-displacement machines, the handlebar shape was reminiscent of Buddha's eyebrow, which Honda personally saw as a selling point. By April 1960, however, when the number of dealers had increased from fifteen to at least forty, warranty claims on the Dream began to pile up. Diagnosis: leaks, as well as defective clutches. "Within a month, we had improved seals and stronger clutch springs. But what was far more important," recalls the then branch manager, "was the fact that people in town were suddenly interested in our Super Cub."

THE IDEA: LESS IS IN FACT SOMETIMES MORE

While 27,000 of them were already rolling off the production line every month in Japan, where production had been moved from Saitama to Suzaka for capacity reasons, at first hardly anyone in the US took any notice of the everyday vehicle with its fully enclosed chain, leg shield, and semiautomatic three-speed transmission. "Admittedly, advertising was limited almost exclusively to the larger Hondas, as we believed that the Cub would damage our image in the US macho motorcycle market," Kawashima explains today.

After initial inquiries from the Sears department store chain, which already distributed Vespa and Puch in the US, the first Cub models then frequently found their way not into the showrooms of motorcycle dealers but into the displays of a wide variety of sports and leisure stores. Under the direction of sales manager Jack McCormack, who unceremoniously sent his people out in El Camino trucks loaded with Super Cub and Dream motorcycles in search of dealers, the number of dealerships quickly rose to 125 in the western United States. Now that the Pico Boulevard branch was finally seeing significant sales, the advertising budget was increased to $20,000 in 1960 and $150,000 the following year.

Even before Honda hired the well-known advertising agency Grey Advertising in 1962 and the advent of its legendary advertising campaign with the catchy slogan "You meet the nicest people on a Honda," the Super Cub made its way into magazines such as *Time* and *Life*, but also *Playboy* and the tabloids of the day. And a resourceful dealer had also discovered that the four-stroke lightweight did not necessarily need to have asphalt under its 17-inch wheels.

Herb Uhl, a dealer from Idaho, thought his son Bill, who had made his first off-road attempts on a 125 cc two-stroke Harley the year before, could do without the leg shield and chain case. The boy got along excellently with the Super Cub, so the plastic was taken off, and Herb also removed the turn signals and handlebar fairing without further ado. He also took care of the exhaust – the one-piece thing was much too long for off-road use, and he screwed an aluminum plate under the engine to protect it from stone chips. The most important thing, however, seemed to him to be the transmission. The small stock sprocket on the rear wheel was replaced with a luscious seventy-two-tooth sprocket that a good friend and expert had worked on with great care on the lathe and mill. Last but not least, the road tires were replaced with knobby tires.

Herb Uhl from Idaho is considered the originator of all off-road Hondas. It's no wonder that Honda placed his quote in the center of early advertising brochures: "The Honda is quite simply every sportsman's best friend," he explained.

Bill Uhl, now a well-known six-day and off-road racer, was the first to ride a "stripped-down" C 100 in off-road competition in 1960.

THE 50 BECOMES THE 55

Just one year later, all Cub models were modified. While the electric starter made the CA 102 comfort version even easier to operate, the off-road version was now called the Trail 55. With a 2 mm increase in bore, the displacement of the OHV engine was now 54 cc, thus making it suitable for highway use according to the registration regulations. The engine now produced 5 hp at 9,500 rpm, and the fuel tank was also increased in size to 1.5 gallons. Those who didn't need the lush mountain gearing could also unscrew the seventy-two-tooth outer ring of the split sprocket and place the chain on the remaining inner forty-two-tooth sprocket common on the C 100. The year before, all Cub models had already received the new modified frame, which now did without the elaborate front engine mount. At the same time, a new, centrally positioned clutch adjustment mechanism had been introduced to facilitate adjustment.

Cycle World tested a Trail 55 for the first time in November, praising not only the cleverly designed centrifugal clutch but also the brake lever for the rear brake, which was mounted on the left of the handlebar in addition to the foot pedal and could thus be operated either by hand or foot. The only criticism was the narrow handlebars. "Although it seems well suited for slow motorcycle cruising, we would have liked a wider one when our enthusiasm outstripped our clear mind and we temporarily forgot that we were, after all, at full speed," the test editor quipped.

The next model update, which was due not only to customer requests but also to an official decree, was due in 1964. Instead of the short, bottom-mounted exhaust muffler, the newly designed exhaust system was raised and fitted with two extra heat shields. To prevent the danger of forest fires caused by flying sparks, the exhaust was fitted with a carbon particle atomizer, the so-called spark arrestor, which was already required by forestry regulations at the time.

Not only did the then-ten-year-old Bill Uhl win his first off-road competition on the modified Cub, but customers also found the little Uhl-modified Honda to be just what had been missing there in Podunk Boise. They wanted one too. When they were on the farm or hunting, these customers didn't care if the thing could go 30 or 40 miles per hour, and Uhl soon didn't know what to do with all the plastic parts he was unscrewing day after day.

His niche in the market, meanwhile, didn't go unnoticed for long. One evening in the late summer of 1960, Jack McCormack was puzzled as to why country bumpkins from Idaho were so keen on the Super Cub. By phone, Uhl explained why his fellow Idahoans were clamoring for his reconfigured Super Cubs. The numbers didn't lie; his Boise sales alone were more than fifty times what the six Los Angeles Honda dealers were showing. McCormack was thrilled, and Kawashima's feedback to Japan happened without much delay, resulting in a Trail 50 being offered from the factory as early as 1961. Officially called the CA 100 T, the newcomer was priced at $275, only $30 more than the basic model with leg shield and dual seat.

Even divers could easily transport their equipment to the water's edge with the 55, as the advertising wants to convey (*left*). TV producer Bill Holmes's hunting buddies include not only his vehicle but also his Weatherby Mark V (*below*).

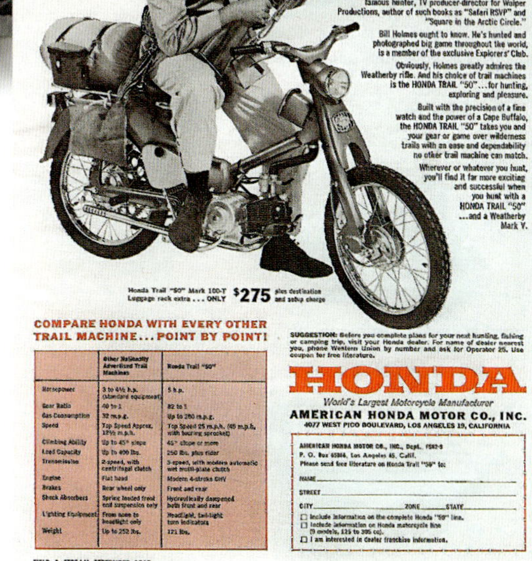

	Other Nationally Advertised Trail Machines	Honda Trail "50"
Horsepower	3 to 4½ h.p. (standard equipment)	5 h.p.
Gear Ratio	40 to 1	82 to 1
Gas Consumption	32 m.p.g.	Up to 200 m.p.g.
Speed	Top Speed Approx. 12½ m.p.h.	Top Speed 25 m.p.h. (45 m.p.h. with touring sprocket)
Climbing Ability	Up to 45° slope	45° slope or more
Load Capacity	Up to 400 lbs.	250 lbs. plus rider
Transmission	2-speed, with centrifugal clutch	3-speed, with modern automatic wet multi-plate clutch
Engine	Flat head	Modern 4-stroke OHV
Brakes	Rear wheel only	Front and rear
Shock Absorbers	Spring loaded front coil suspension only	Hydraulically dampened both front and rear
Lighting Equipment	From none to headlight only	Headlight, tail-light turn indicators
Weight	Up to 252 lbs.	121 lbs.

Naturally, the Trail 55 was seamlessly integrated into Grey Advertising's advertising campaign. With an advertising budget of three million dollars, Honda began running primetime television spots in 1964. Ads for the Trail 55 were now also placed in special-interest magazines, such as *Field & Stream* and other outdoor magazines, most of which featured hunters on steep slopes – of course with smiles on their faces; the filled, optional rifle mount on the handlebars; and the bagged game on the wide luggage rack.

RECOGNIZING SUCCESS: HONDA REWARDED DEALERSHIPS WITH THE HIGHEST SALES WITH CHROMED TRAIL 55 AND 90 "DEALER SPECIALS."

Who needs a pickup truck to go camping? Early ads may have been small, but they were effective. Where is the nearest Honda dealer? A call to Western Union will tell you; just ask for Operator 25.

AS YOU LIKE IT: MORE DISPLACEMENT, MORE GEARS

1964 upgrade: The CT 90 now had four gears, a 90 cc engine, and more horsepower. It also had the USDA Forest Service spark arrestor to prevent misfires from causing forest fires.

When it was decided in Japan to develop a higher-displacement model with 90 cc alongside the 50, the end of the Trail 55 was in sight. A new engine, still an OHV unit with cast-steel cylinder head, was quickly developed. With a bore of 49 mm and a stroke of 46 millimeters, the CT 200 unit produced 6.5 hp at 7,500 rpm. The magneto ignition had now given way to a more powerful battery and coil ignition system, as had already been fitted to the two-cylinder models, but also to the C 102 with electric starter. Instead of three gears, the driver now had four gear ratios at his disposal: 25.2, 16, 11.8, and 9.5, respectively. For the oil supply, the engine development team led by Daiji Hoshino had resorted to a conventional oil pump instead of centrifugal lubrication, the pump itself sitting in the left half of the engine behind the DC alternator. The chassis of the new CT 200 had been reinforced, and the now-undisguised handlebars were adjustable. Thanks to the relatively steep steering head angle of 26.5 degrees, the wheelbase of the Trail 55's successor was 46.8 inches (1,188 mm), just under 1 cm more than that of a normal Super Cub, not least thanks to the engine, which weighed 55.1 pounds (25 kg). The rider's footrests were profiled and hinged, and the "skid plate," which was still open at the front on the predecessor and was intended to protect the engine from stone chips or similar objects, now sat between two chrome-plated protective brackets bolted to the top of the steering head.

From mid-1964, the CT 200—or Trail 90, as it was called in all advertisements—was available for $330, as always in a choice of scarlet red or yellow. In the meantime, the entire Honda model range had grown to fifteen models, and the branch had moved to Gardena, 100 West Alondra—and not just due to a lack of space. Every second new motorcycle sold in the US was a Honda. Honda sold about 8,000 vehicles per month and had expanded its dealer network well eastward. While the CT 200, which now managed just under 60 mph with the street transmission, sold brilliantly and inspired bands such as the Hondells to sing about the "Little Honda," the Honda engineers were already planning their next coup. In addition to developing the CB 450, which made all Triumph, BSA, and company products look ancient, they continued to tinker with the horizontal single-cylinder engines. A general conversion of the existing engine range to OHC control, together with an alloy cylinder head, was intended to ensure long-term sales success and satisfied customers for the small single-cylinder models. In Germany, where Honda could report only modest sales figures with the C 110 and C 100, a wooden model of the future 50 cc OHC unit was displayed in 1964. But since Honda was primarily concerned with the Black Bomber at the time, it was a good two years before the European clientele in general and those who were flirting with a Trail 90 got to see the new models.

In the meantime, all kinds of accessory companies were also making an effort to supply Honda customers with things that were not available from the dealer. For example, those who were fed up with greasy hands when converting from the 40 road to the 68 off-road gear ratio could screw the "Go-Matic" from the Palo Alto–based company Ampico onto the swing arm for $55.

Thanks to an extra shaft with three gears, the outer two of which were connected either to the small or the large sprocket on the rear wheel, the Trail 90 rider could select the desired gearing by means of a cable on the handlebars and switch back and forth between "high" and "low" range.

The idea of the dual-range transmission was, of course, also adapted by other accessory manufacturers for competitors of the Trail 90. Honda itself had long since addressed this shortcoming when the first Trail 90s of the 1966 model year were in dealers' showrooms. With its alloy cylinder head, modified OHC engine concept, new carburetor, and improved transmission, the new engine was significantly quieter than its OHV predecessor, although the bore and stroke of the OHC unit were the same as its predecessor, and power had increased from 6.5 to 7 hp at 8,500 rpm. The power unit, which was also installed in the new, sporty CL, SL, and S 90 models, remained in this form for only a few months on the Trail 90, which was now officially called the CT 90 rather than the CT 200. In the middle of the 1967 model year, starting with chassis number 122551, Honda surprised its customers with the so-called "posi-torque" transmission.

The inconspicuous but effective dual-range transmission, which further shortened the four "normal" gear ratios (2.538/1.611/1.190/0.958) by a ratio of 1.867, was located on the left in front of the previous transmission output shaft and made the sixty-eight-tooth sprocket superfluous. The driver could now easily switch from the on-road to the off-road ratio via a "speed range selector" on the left crankcase cover.

The swing-arm-mounted Go-Matic was available for the Trail 55 as well as for the CT 200 and offered cable-operated switching from off-road to on-road gearing.

MODEL UPDATES: THE METAMORPHOSIS INTO THE ALL-ROUNDER

The CT 90 was immediately given the suffix K0 and was offered unchanged with this clever idea until the end of 1968. Instead of the short swing arm typical of the Super Cub, the revised K1 guided its front wheel from 1969 onward via a telescopic fork from the CL 90 parts store; at the same time, the induction tract was relocated over the left side of the engine.

The increased ground clearance (6.9 inches [175 mm] instead of 5.4 inches [137 mm]) had a positive effect off-road. Plastic trim on the main frame tube provided a sportier look, and the next year, pickup truck owners and campers who wanted to strap their CT to the front or rear of their vehicle were delighted.

The little Honda was not just a musical theme for the Beach Boys. The studio group the Hondells also recorded the Honda advertising song "You Meet the Nicest People on a Honda" in 1965. "Little Honda" stayed on the charts for four weeks starting in late November 1964.

The engine of the CT 200, available from 1964, was based on the CM 90's OHV unit. In 1965, a gear was added to the transmission, the handlebar was now no longer covered but could be adjusted in the direction of travel, and the 90 on the emblem under the headlight was still found to one side.

Starting in 1969, the short swing arm was replaced by a telescopic fork. A new position for the carburetor was also added, and there was a quick release on the upper triple clamp for easier transport. Customers in Montana were pleased with the high-altitude setting on the Keihin carburetor.

From then on, the handlebars could be turned 90 degrees to the left or right by means of a quick-release system. The turn signals were also new, because in the eight states of California, Georgia, Kansas, Maine, Massachusetts, Nevada, New Hampshire, and Oregon, turn signals were already required by the respective Departments of Motor Vehicles (DMV).

Honda responded to customer requests from the Rocky Mountains and Montana starting in 1970. In order to compensate for the overrich air-fuel mixture at high altitudes, a modified jet kit would undoubtedly have sufficed, but Honda, in view of the sales figures, went whole hog and equipped the new round slide carburetor from chassis number 000001A with a mixture compensation unit. An extra pull knob, which Honda said should be pulled at altitudes above 6,000 feet above sea level, released by negative pressure holes with calibrated auxiliary jets on the main and idle jets, again ensuring proper mixture composition.

In the same year, the previously profiled footrests were again replaced by ones with detent rubbers. Beginning in 1972, an auxiliary tank, which held 0.2 gallons (0.8 liters) and was mounted on the left under the luggage rack, increased the CT's range, but also its weight to 200 pounds (91 kg). For easier shifting, the previous shift sequence (down to shift up) was reversed on the K6 version in 1975. The year before, the Trail had already received brake-wear indicators and an emergency stop switch on the throttle grip.

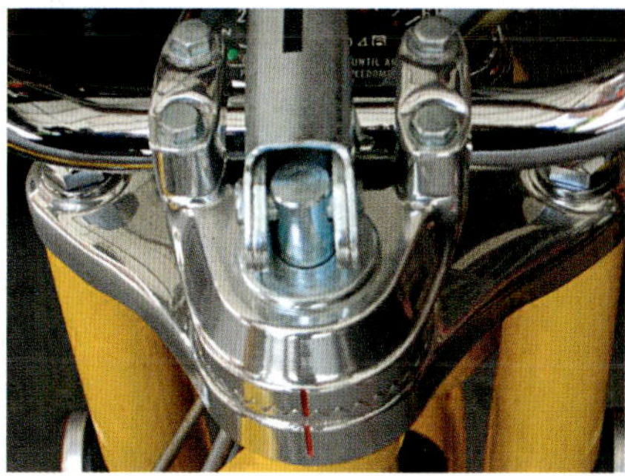

CT-90 K5
CT-70 K3

Full-page ads featuring the CT always showed "action" to make clear what was possible with the Trail 90. The rare CT 50 (*below*) had a three-speed dual-range transmission, but it was sold only in Asia in the late 1960s.

Honda shapes the world of wheels—with the emphasis on the word "shapes." With special kits, the entire C series became even more attractive; four body styles were available to choose from and were intended to spice up the home-baked Super Cub for the youth market.

US SPECIAL CONVERSIONS: SUITCASE CYCLES AND THE RALLY CUSTOM GROUP

As the sales figures of the standard Cub models slowly declined at the end of the 1960s, a new market strategy was tried out with the Rally Custom Group. Kits for the CM 90 and 91, and also for the C 100 and C 102, were intended to make them more visually attractive to would-be racers. Four kits were offered: Boss, Rally, Roadster, and Student. The kits included special tanks, seats, speedometers, handlebars, and – if necessary – cables and switches as well. However, the whole thing was more of a flop than a success. The Student kits, for example, were offered to dealers for as little as $5 in 1969 but did not make the standard Cubs any more likely to sell. Most customers preferred to go for the Trail, SL, and XL models. Today, vehicles with this kit equipment are rare and coveted.

The Suitcase Cycle was a small step-through motorcycle modification designed by Lawrence Shapiro for rapid breakdown and compact transport by general aviation aircraft, as well as land and sea transport. This involved sawing up the frames and fitting them with quick-release devices. "The S&K company began in 1967 in my father's garage in Westchester, California," says Shapiro's son Jeff. "Thanks to rapid growth and positive feedback from pilots who otherwise would not have been mobile in some places, our Suitcase Cycle was the perfect answer."

For private planes, breakdown bikes go easily through the usual small doors.

You disconnect the entire electrical system by means of a simple pull-apart connector.

Twist this handle and the frame separates. Modified frame is stronger than original.

with This Cycle in a Suitcase

about a minute longer. To achieve these quick-change capabilities, S & K added 90 new parts and modified 12 others.

These Hondas not only tear down quickly, they reduce into very small units. Without cases they will fit through openings as small as 12½ inches by 21 inches. This allows storage in small aircraft baggage compartments like those on the Cessna 172 and 182. Detachable handlebars, folding foot pegs and brake levers, modified gas tanks, and quick-release seat brackets make such compression possible. None of these modifications weakens the bikes or adversely affects their handling characteristic.

Prices start at $398, from S & K Air Sea Cycles, 1257 South La Brea, Inglewood, Calif.—*Jim Davis.*

In the early 1970s, the company moved to Santa Monica Airport and soon had twelve employees, including Jeff and his brother Greg. In its prime, the company modified all sorts of motorcycles for airline transport, including various Suzuki 100s and 125s, and a 185, in addition to the Honda CT 90, which was considered the top seller. "For Honda, it was the CT 90, CL 100, as well as the SL 125," Jeff explains. Approximately 1,000 vehicles were prepared and converted in this way until 1974, when it was over—for product liability reasons, as one can surely understand. Brochures and advertisements from that time often show the Suitcase Cycles in motion, with some showing how to disassemble a vehicle in five minutes and stow it in a Cessna, Beechcraft, Piper, or Mooney. Accessories included hard cases, as well as soft bags and crash helmets.

FROM THE CT 90 COMES THE CT 110

The Trail CT's displacement remained unchanged for sixteen years, then increased to 105 cc—for greater torque and versatility.

The CT did not undergo any further drastic modifications until 1980, when the engine was enlarged to 105 cc. For this purpose, not only was the cylinder bored out to 52 mm (2 inches), but the stroke was also lengthened from 45.6 to 49.5 mm (1.8 to 1.95 inches). The engine now produced 7.6 hp, but it was much more resilient and required only 7,500 revs to reach rated power. The entire electrical system was 12 volt, and even the ignition was now electronic. This was also the case with the C 70, which was relaunched on the US market as the C 70 Passport starting in 1981.

In this first model year, the CT, thus strengthened, actually did not have the dual-range transmission. In the US, the import of the CT 110 was finally discontinued in 1986, since the popular Honda could no longer be registered for public road traffic due to environmental regulations. In Canada, however, and especially in Australia, sales of the CT 110 continued—particularly thanks to the Australian postal service, which imported a handsome number each year for its mailmen.

Unbelievable, but true: In 1995, the Honda CT 110 was also sold in Germany for one season. A small secondary importer in Trier offered the Honda, which was equipped for use in Australia with a closed chain case and two (!) side stands, for just under 4,000 marks—probably on the assumption that, thanks to recently changed driver's license regulations, Class 3 owners would pick something different instead of one of the usual 125 cc scooters. But, as with the Honda Super Cub four decades earlier, German customers unfortunately didn't play ball.

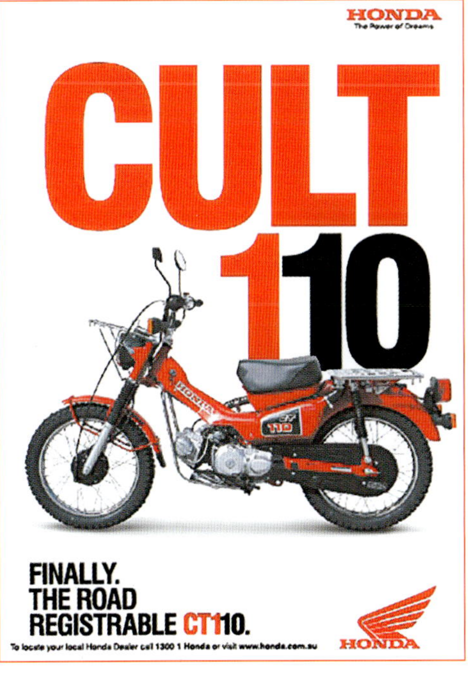

In Australia, the CT 110 became the "postie bike," but without the dual-range transmission, and—as with the original Cub—again with a closed chain case. For several years, only an "agri-cultural version" was publicly sold, and only in the first few years of the twenty-first century was there again a road-legal CT 110 for everyone.

FROM THE FARM IN NEW ZEALAND TO MUNICH

I saw a yellow Trail 90 at the Stafford Show in 1995, and at that time I still believed it was a crazy conversion, of which there were more than enough in England. When my buddy Paul, a crane operator in Brisbane, sent me an email with a picture of his "postie bike" years later, I asked him to keep an eye out for a CT for me. In 2004, he found one—at Casbolts Honda in Christchurch, New Zealand. The Honda came to me via sea container. Not much could be done to it, but the work piled up. The bearings in the front wheel were gone, the tank was leaking, and the electronics had a serious ground problem. Finally, an ugly side stand mount that the previous owner had "fried" had to be removed. As for the parts: in retrospect, thanks to some well-stocked dealers such as Beatrice Cycle in Nebraska, Classic Motorcycle Supplies (www.cmsnl.com) in the Netherlands, and—last but not least—eBay, it was relatively easy to get the CT 90—probably used only as a pure "farm bike" in New Zealand—completely fit and registered again.

Uwe's CT has a chrome shield on the main exhaust pipe and a handlebar quick-release switch to turn the handlebar 90 degrees. The bend in the exhaust pipe has no heat shield here.

The differently mounted 5.5-liter tank has a tank cap under the short one-man seat. The small auxiliary tank is located on the left rear and held in place by means of a snap lock; it was available from 1982 onward and has a capacity of 2.3 liters.

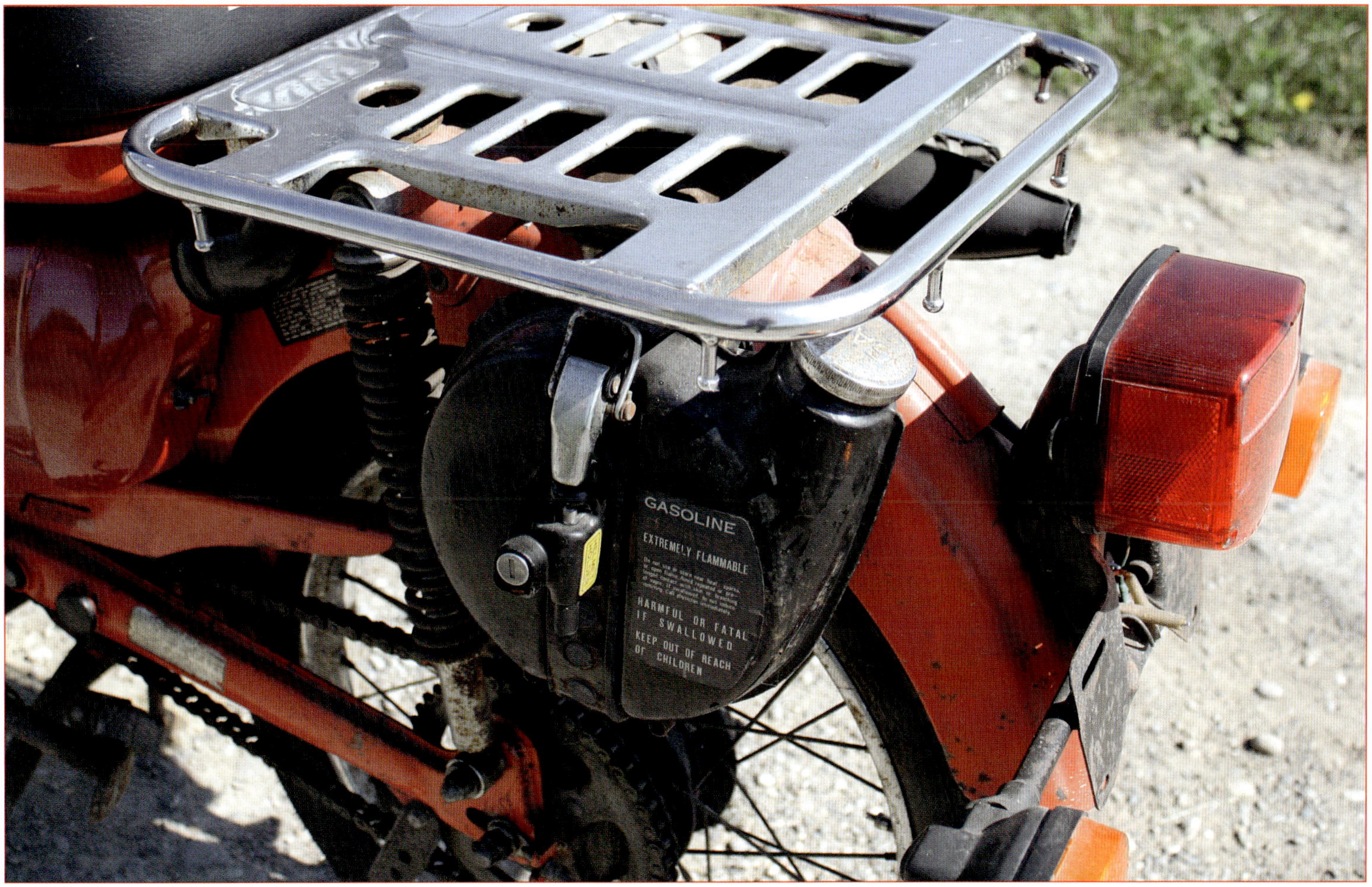

Who can sleep, with the CT selling like hotcakes? At the same time, Yamaha was offering the YG 1T Trailmaster, with manually adjusted dual-range gearing, and in the early 1960s the Omaha Trail, like the 55 without a front fender. Hodaka, a US-Japanese merger, introduced the ACE 90 in 1964. The off-road machine produced 8.25 hp.

OFF-ROAD FLEA CIRCUS

Of course, the success of the Honda Trail 50 did not remain hidden from the competition in the US for long. As early as 1962, Yamaha offered the Omaha Trail 50, a light motorcycle with a similar step-through concept. The little two-stroke bike could be purchased for $285, and even the small rotary valve engine produced 5 hp. It had a three-speed gearbox with a double gear rim on the rear wheel, and it could even be started easily with a press of the thumb. However, Yamaha sold the YG 1 much more successfully and in 1964 also produced a Trailmaster variant of the 80, the YG1-T.

Harley-Davidson, which had been associated with the Italian Aermacchi factories since the beginning of the 1960s, purchased small two-stroke models such as the M 50 for "badge engineering." Equipped with a manual three-speed transmission, these models were aimed at a similar clientele but admittedly did not offer anything like the range of action of the Trail 50. From 1966, Suzuki relied on the successor to the KT 15, called the KT 120 Bear Cat, which also offered a dual-range transmission beginning in 1968. From the mid-1960s, however, real off-road sport freaks opted for machines such as the Hodaka Ace 90, on which powerful riders such as Gordon Sechler and Larry Yount won the National Trail Race or the exceptionally difficult Dry Creek Trail in the fall of 1965. To be sure, Kawasaki was also in the mix of light off-road machines. In the early 1970s, its advertising agency fought with a particularly pointed pen to duly emphasize the name of the new G4TR Trail Boss: "If the Honda Trail 90 had 10-speed transmission, it would be almost as good as the Kawasaki Trail Boss, except it still wouldn't have: 11.5 horsepower, double loop tube frame, Superlube automatic oil injection, and 12,000-mile or 12-month warranty, or that 10-speed transmission."

A CAREER DOWN UNDER

At the beginning of the 1980s, the Australian and New Zealand postal services began importing the Honda CT 90 and its successor, the CT 110, for their letter carriers, the "posties." As a result, the "postie bike" quickly established itself there and eventually morphed into the bestselling motorcycle in Australia and New Zealand. While the CT 110 P was delivered without a dual-range transmission and was retired after a few years and sold only in public auctions to private individuals, the CT 110 AG was sold for a time only as a vehicle without road registration. Beginning in the middle of 2009, both CT 110 versions were offered with road registration at a cost of 3,490 Australian dollars.

Although its postal career Down Under is probably over for environmental reasons, the CT 110 remains one of Australia's most popular motorcycles. Clubs and events attest to this.

Numerous clubs and interest groups still organize so-called Postie Bike Challenges, with some of the groups maintaining an online presence. Nathan Millward rode his postie from Sydney to London; his book *Going Postal* was published in February 2011.

MD

晴れても雨でも、そして雪の日にも毎日お手紙を届けてくれる

真っ赤なスーパーカブ。

働くスーパーカブの代表選手

スーパーカブはいろいろな現場で活躍する働くバイクの代名詞でもある。
中でもホンダと郵政省の共同開発によって誕生した、郵便配達専用のMDシリーズはその極みといえよう。
郵政省から日本郵便へと母体は変わっても、毎日お手紙を配達してくれるのは
真っ赤なスーパーカブに乗った郵便屋さん。
郵政博物館所蔵の写真と最新モデルで、ちょっとだけ赤いスーパーカブを振り返る。

ALL ABOUT SUPER CUB

A workhorse for Japan's delivery heroes: The MD was made extra sturdy and also served as a template for the Press Cub. The 14-inch wheels were later adopted for the Little Cub.

JAPANESE COUNTERPART—THE MD SERIES

As early as the 1960s, when Japanese postmen were probably getting tired of their bicycles, the Postal Ministry discussed with motorcycle manufacturers the production of a postal moped specially tailored for Japan. And yes, Honda got the nod. Development began in 1967; for this, more logically, the OHC engine was used, which had more pep and allowed higher revs. Initially, only a large rear rack was added and the headlight was set higher. But it wasn't done yet; after initial field tests and further improvements, the first MDs were then introduced nationwide beginning in 1971.

Based on the Super Cub 90, the MD had a telescopic fork and conventional motorcycle handlebars without fairing. Probably the biggest difference compared to the standard Cub was the smaller and wider 14-inch wheels. Depending on the location, a carburetor preheater or heated grips were also fitted. In 1973, an MD 50 was launched in addition to the MD 90. Year after year, small improvements were made, and although the MD is no longer so common in Japan today, numerous letter carriers still use it. The speedometer was integrated into the headlight as usual, while the luggage rack—mounted above the front wheel—was designed to be extremely sturdy so that bags or containers could be loaded easily. A sufficiently large distance between the wheel and the mudguard was important.

The MD was available as MD 50, MD 90, and MD 110, also Yūbin Cub or Yūsei Cub, all painted in the usual postal service red. But the MD's days are numbered; according to a recent report in the *Japan Times*, the postal service intends to exchange all the 85,000 delivery vehicles for electric scooters in the long term. Collectors and private individuals can rejoice, because these "discarded" MDs will then be sold.

For roughing it: The side stand on the swing arm has an extra extension arm and is virtually indestructible.

Z-50A K5
QA-50 K2
HONDA
HONDA

QA-50 K2. Here's a mighty little mini that every youngster will be delighted to ride! Better looking than ever, the Honda "Q" sports a sleek, redesigned fuel tank and attractive new fender striping. It's a little bike that won't be missed, because it stands out from the mini crowd—which is why it's so popular with the mini bunch!

And the QA-50 K2 has a host of features that makes it easy to handle. Features like better steering stability and a low, easy-riding seat. The handlebars swivel so it can be easily transported to the family campsite. Front and rear brakes as on big bikes.

For safety, there's a handy ignition cutoff switch right on the handlebars. And a Honda spark arrestor/muffler for riding in the woods. And its economical little four-stroke OHC engine is quieter than other minis—very important to fellow campers! When a youngster yearns for a minibike, there's only one way to go—in the direction of your nearest Honda dealer's. That's where the fun begins. And because it's a Honda, that's where it keeps on going!

Specifications on the Honda QA-50 K2

Engine
- Type .... Four-stroke, single-cylinder
- Displacement 49cc
- Bore and Stroke .... 42.0 mm x 35.6 mm
- Compression Ratio 8.5:1

Transmission .... Two-speed, constant mesh
Clutch .... Wet, multi-plate automatic
Brakes .... Internal expanding shoe
Suspension .... Front, telescopic fork; Rear, rigid
Tire Size .... Front, 4.00-5; Rear, 4.00-5
Ignition System .... Flywheel magneto
Starting System .... Kick starter

Dimensions and Capacities
- Wheelbase ... 34.4 in.
- Dry weight ... 84 lbs.
- Overall length ... 47.2 in.
- Overall width ... 24.0 in.
- Seat height ... 22.8 in.
- Fuel capacity ... 1.2 gal.

Color .... Candy orange

All specifications subject to change without notice.
"K" numbers in Honda model designations indicate model changes.

Open here for your own Z-50A K3 mini-poster.

HONDA QA 50

All good things come in threes, so after the success of the Z 50A and the ST and CT series in the US, the Japanese decided to follow up with another minibike. The QA 50 hit the market in 1970 and was not intended for street use, which is why the smallest of all Honda models did not have a light system.

The engine was scaled to the dimensions of the C 50/Monkey/Dax generation, but unusually it was OHV-controlled and had just gears, which were engaged as usual by a rocker shift lever. Both cylinder and head, however, were newly developed, matching the bore and stroke (42 × 35.6 mm) of the short-stroke top end of a moped model, the PC 50, which was sold in Belgium, the Netherlands, Luxembourg, and England, as well as in South America. The 5-inch wheels were guided at the front by an undamped telescopic fork, and the powered rear wheel sat rigidly in the tubular frame. Plastic mudguards shielded against dust and dirt thrown up by the 4-inch-wide tires, and the high handlebar was equipped with a hard rubber toggle on the upper triple clamp, with which it could be easily folded down for transport. The QA did not have a foot brake lever—both brakes were operated manually by Bowden cable. The K0 of the first model year was followed in 1974 by the K1, with a chrome tank and white mudguards.

The QA 50's top speed was just under 31 mph (50 kph), and it had a well-hidden exhaust—with the Krizman Spark Arrestor required in the US. In 1974, the QA was discontinued after the K4 model. The minibike was never sold in Europe.

The modular system sends its regards: The QA combined the advantages of the Z 50 A with those of the PC/PS 50 machines. Headlights or taillights were not necessary, since road approval was not an issue.

DAX
HONDA
ST-50

RE-
ISSUED
AND RE-
DESIGNED

Turning old into new: Honda has restyling down pat.

MARKETS AND PRICES CHANGED IN THE 1980s. AND, OF COURSE, SO DID HONDA'S RANGE OF MODELS FOR YOUNG PEOPLE.

Making good things even better: on the CTs, the conversion to 12-volt electrics was a sensible improvement.

On the topic of maintenance and potential savings on the ST 50: the throttle cable was now routed outside and more accessible, and there was a better, oil-damped telescopic fork and less chrome on the exhaust.

DAX HONDA

THE AB-23 SERIES RECEIVED A NEAT MAIN STAND, TURN SIGNALS, A REVISED REAR, AND A BETTER-MOUNTED CAMSHAFT. BUT THERE WERE ALSO UNPLEASANT SURPRISES FOR HOBBY TUNERS, WHICH THE ANTIMANIPULATION CATALOG PRESCRIBED.

The ZB with an aluminum frame was supposed to embody the spirit of the time, but it was not a sales success.

Although neither the ST 70 nor the smaller-displacement ST 50 was offered in central Europe from 1980 onward, a Japanese Dax version (still called the ST 50) was in the Honda lineup in Greece from 1979 onward under the name ST 70 M.

A new, revised styling made this Dax special. Its typical look now featured a megaphone-shaped exhaust. The new 70s also had three-star rims instead of the previously common four-star ones—which admittedly came from the parts rack of the replacement CY 50. Known in Japan as the "Naughty Dax," this model was identifiable by a front mudguard bolted to the bottom, and the new seat was now a banana-shaped chopper seat with a luggage rack. The power unit was the four-speed engine with manual clutch.

For the US market, Honda continued to produce the CT 70, which was popular for off-road use. It hardly looked like an ST 70 any longer, however, although some basic parts such as the frame and engine remained the same. In order to refine the off-road capability both visually and practically, the mudguards had been made of plastic since 1979 and were also mounted much higher on the front fork. The future CT 70 series was based on this design and was produced by Honda until 1996. Honda did not have a single competitor for a long time, until Yamaha launched a similarly cuddly off-road model, the Chappy, in 1981.

Honda tried to make up for its Dax abstinence in the early 1980s with the CY 50. The four-stroke with the upright cylinder had been developed for the CB 50; in Germany, the four-speed engine with conventional manual clutch received the tame camshaft, which, with a correspondingly small carburetor cross section, lowered engine output to a feeble 2.1 hp. That came to an end in 1986—and suddenly a revised ST model arrived at the Honda dealer with some technically high-quality novelties as a treat for the sixteen-year-olds. This new edition was given the name AB 23 and was also offered again in Europe. In addition to its improved 12-volt electrical system and ball-bearing camshaft, it also had a number of optical innovations to offer. The front fork finally had serious damping, and there was a plastic mud flap on the rear mudguard.

The high-mounted exhaust was painted black in keeping with the times, and the heat shield now had holes instead of ribs. The turn signals were larger, square, flexibly mounted, and made of plastic. The new model was available in candy red, candy blue, and silver paint colors. A new 70 cc version unfortunately made it only into the French Honda sales program.

Only a year later, the Honda Monkey ZB and Monkey R/RT were launched as representatives of the new minibike generation. Analogous to the then-current super sport machines, they were built around a welded aluminum Deltabox frame, and the rear wheel was mounted on a swing arm with a central shock absorber.

The minibikes still rolled on 8-inch wheels, but they appeared larger overall and nowhere near as delicate as their predecessors—which ultimately also diminished their popularity. The Monkey ZB and R were available in red and white, the RT in metallic blue.

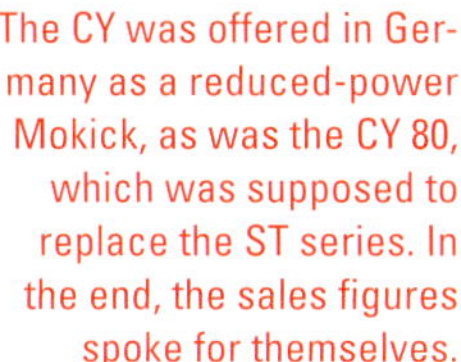

The CY was offered in Germany as a reduced-power Mokick, as was the CY 80, which was supposed to replace the ST series. In the end, the sales figures spoke for themselves.

In August 1991, Soichiro Honda passed away at the age of eighty five. In the same year, a slightly modified ST 50 appeared, the successor to the AB 23. It was in mourning, one might say, with a black-painted engine, a black exhaust, colored mudguards, white rims, and new decoration. Available color options were red, white, and black. The manufacturer did not make any further technical changes or improvements.

In 1996 the last generation of the new AB 23 ST 50 was produced. This time, to honor customer wishes, it seemed that the company had strategically returned to classic and nostalgic designs. These models were again equipped with chrome guards, a silver engine block, and rims of the same color, but they still had a black exhaust and chrome heat shield. The colors were again classic candy red and candy blue, and the decoration was kept rather nondescript. These last ST-50 and ST-70 variants were still produced and sold for Europe until 1999, and then it was finally over. While unlikely, it may still be possible to find a brand-new model at a Honda dealer today. But if not, determined enthusiasts should certainly still be able to at least find a bike imported from Japan.

The Z 50 J was also further modified for the Japanese market during the 1980s and '90s as the Gorilla, then later also as the Baja, with a buffalo tank but one-piece handlebars, war paint, and twin headlights. The CT 70 was finally sold in the US beginning in the 1990s, without folding handlebar halves.

MY HONDA STORY

ALMOST LIKE LEGO . . .

Marijn Engels was fascinated by the Honda modular system, which is why he has often given the Hondas he restores a little of his own design. The Dutch art director and blogger is part of the lively Honda scene in his home country, where a colorful hodgepodge of these vehicles can be found alongside the Dax and Monkey.

My Honda story logically also starts with the classic saying "You meet the nicest people" . . . because it's true. I have tried it out. Thanks to their reliability, the little bikes take you to exotic places—far away. Fortunately, Honda's horizontal single cylinders have many parts that can be interchanged; I know this because I've been riding such lightweights since I was sixteen. And although I have a CB 1100 in my garage, I'm in a good mood every time I ride one of the little Hondas.

My first Honda was an SS 50, which I worked on and improved. In Holland, the SS—with its five gears and four-stroke engine—was already a real motorcycle for a sixteen-year-old . . . or at least close to it. Since then, I've owned many more of these little Hondas; I also particularly liked the Z 50, on its 8-inch wheels, and the ST 50, on 10-inch wheels. And I still have both of them in the garage. When I was a teenager, these tiny bikes really represented something original. The few that were officially sold here in Holland were not marketed as mopeds but as motorcycles—the law clearly stipulated that. But hundreds of teenagers made their own rules, found a loophole, and insured them as mopeds in the Netherlands. It is important to know that mopeds did not have a normal license plate requirement at that time.

I also often went over to England to buy vehicles and parts for the C 70 and C 90—of course for vehicles I had at home. And so, all sorts of things came out of it, often the classic wolf in sheep's clothing. My creations often carried me, my tent, and other camping gear to France and sometimes over to Spain, England, or even Germany. Others had to take the bus to their vacation spots. I often made friends with other riders who also saw the Honda as something like a ticket to freedom or a means of transportation to adventure.

C50

The popularity of the step-through range of Honda machines is legendary. More of these machines have been sold around the world than any other single design from the beginning of motorcycling. The C50 is the ideal utility bike, with a 49cc engine.

C90

Top of the popular step-through range, the C90 offers improved engine performance from the same proven basic design, with smooth ride, dependable brakes and protective leg shields. Easy to ride, and easy to maintain.

C70

The C70 is the 72cc version of the step-through range, with an air cooled O.H.C. 4 stroke single cylinder engine, offering all the advantages of the C50 with a larger engine size.

The ZZ model, part of the C series, was given a new shift sequence—all gears down. In everyday use, however, many vehicles proved particularly susceptible to rust on the rear part of the bike.

Left: In the Netherlands, the CD 50R, which was offered in the early 1970s, was considered sporty but not super sporty. *Above*: In the US, the Z 50R, perfectly styled for off-road racing, was a big seller right from the start.

1980
C 70

She is a colorful mix of all kinds of Honda parts. I actually built it for short trips, but it was never used for that. It all started with a C 70 frame, built in 1980, to which I then added all sorts of parts I found suitable in looks, comfort, reliability, and speed. My goal was to build something that would look like an original Honda to the layman but that was actually something special. Front forks, shocks, front rack, engine, and wiring harness all are parts from a 90 Cub. The position light under the headlight and the handlebar and cover are from an older C 70. The short solo seat, tank, and rear rack are parts of a Honda CT 90 from the US, and the taillight is from a Honda CB 450 Black Bomber. The speedometer with the white dial I got from a C 50 H, which was built for sale in Holland. All individual components I have pepped up mechanically as well as visually; all screws are newly galvanized. Only the clutch cover has some patina, just to have something where you can still see its real age.

1971
CD 50

The CD 50 was well over thirty years old when I stumbled across it. When I tracked her down, you could still find a Honda in such nearly unused condition. It was complete, including all three of the keys that came with it, the tool kit, and the odd accessories typical of Holland: the mechanical throttle, the pedals, the weird yellow plastic thing on the front fender, a bicycle bell, and—of course—no turn signals. Almost all owners immediately removed the pedals at that time; the things looked hideous and were unnecessary and completely impractical. And most of them added a horn and turn signals.

I bought the CD 50 as a symbol, so to speak, to keep my Honda youth alive. It was cherished and cared for, and it was kept where it was warm, with a new battery and the original tires, until one day it was time for a new owner. It was a bit hard to see it leave—with a happy new owner who didn't quite comprehend that his father had actually bought him a museum piece for everyday adventures.

SS100
NGK
NGK
OIL 0.7L
MILLYARD

THE NOBLE TINKERERS

Make two out of one, and do it perfectly: Noble tinkerer Allen Millyard has already built several SS 100s, and the sound is stunning.

THE SCENE AROUND THE SUPER CUB AND ALL ITS OFFSHOOTS IS CERTAINLY MORE COLORFUL THAN ANY OTHER, AS THE FOLLOWING PAGES CONFIRM. SO IF YOU FIND AN INCOMPLETE EXAMPLE AND WANT TO FINISH BUILDING IT, HERE ARE SOME WACKY BUILDING INSTRUCTIONS—ALL MASTERPIECES ON TWO WHEELS.

Allen demonstrated his finished V-Twin at a classic event in Stafford, central England. Everyone was thrilled.

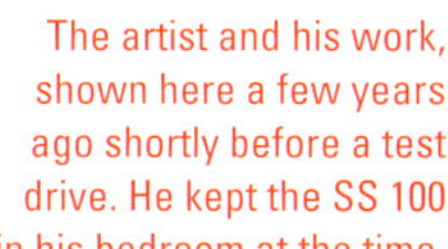
The artist and his work, shown here a few years ago shortly before a test drive. He kept the SS 100 in his bedroom at the time.

Almost finished: to fit the carburetor, parts of the frame had to be modified and notched. This was no easy task.

ENGINEERING ENGINES

It sounds like a Ducati, but it's a shot-glass Honda. At the Classic Mechanics Show in Stafford, central England, years ago, the noble tinkerer Allen Millyard presented a V-Twin based on a Honda SS 50. The idiosyncratic 98 cc Honda is by no means the only one, since Allen has produced several of this species in the meantime.

Now a development engineer at the British Ministry of Defence (MOD), Allen has always been up for "something completely different." At the tender age of fourteen, for example, he installed an 850 cc engine from an Austin Mini in the frame of a well-behaved, two-stroke BSA Bantam (the British equivalent of the DKW RT 125) and rode it around the garden at home. "At the time, my dad just said tersely that I should disassemble the thing as soon as possible, because the narrow wheels, which came from an old Suzuki A 100, could hardly take the weight," the hobbyist recalls. At the age of eighteen, Allen had already gained a lot of experience with a wide variety of machines, including a few Hondas. "At the time, I had built a V-Twin from two Honda C 90 engines. It's fairer to say that it was cobbled together. The thing looked illegal, but it ran, and when I fitted the engine to the chassis of an Italian Malaguti 50, it even managed 80 miles per hour (129 kph)."

"Ten weeks before the Stafford Show in the fall, I needed a real challenge," Allen recalls. "That's when the idea came to me: I wanted to convert a small Honda four-stroke engine into a twin again, but this time I also wanted it to be visually perfect so that it could pass as a 'Honda prototype,' so to speak."

"So, to make a long story short," Allen explains, "I acquired a five-speed SS 50 engine (in the UK, the SS 50 was also available as a four-speed version) and some C 50 Cub three-speed engines to butcher and try out. The biggest problem of the project was the crankshaft, which needed a crankpin that was 14 millimeters (0.55 inches) wider – the second connecting rod had to end somewhere. And, of course, that meant I had to make the case 14 millimeters wider all around. A casing base with chain shaft was cleanly sawed out from a C 50 engine and fitted into the prepared SS 50 housing, after I had measured everything precisely beforehand – a hell of a job, honestly." Since the front cylinder had to be offset from the rear by 14 mm due to the wider bearing journal, the entire chain shaft on the front cylinder also had to be widened – both at the head and on the cylinder itself.

Early projects on the workbench: At the age of eighteen, Allen had already built a Vau engine from two C 90 engines. He widened the housing himself, and a special company was responsible for making the longer crank pin according to his drawing.

A SECOND ATTEMPT WITH MORE AESTHETICS

Allen remembers, "The standing cylinder's oil supply also caused me some headaches. Back then, on the 180 cc engine, I had simply installed oil lines on the outside. Now, however, I routed a 5 mm copper line internally, having previously drilled the appropriate holes in the housing."

After Alpha Bearings, a small business specializing in bearings, fabricated and hardened the longer crankpin for him according to drawings, work began on the crankshaft. It was loosely assembled with the pistons and rings for static balancing, then Allen proceeded to remove metal from both solid cheeks.

Making and timing the camshaft wasn't easy, either. "I made one from two standard camshaft chains," he continues. "I also had to add an extra starting sprocket to the front of the standing cylinder so that the chain would find its way to the camshaft at the right angle and parallel. As for the ignition, I removed the solenoid coil, just like I did on my first one—in its place now sits a second one, 90 degrees off the original breaker, along with its capacitor." Sounds super easy, as Allen tells it.

Nevertheless, it was a load off his mind when the engine gave its first cough at the show in October 1999 and finally ran for the first time—cleanly, without rattling.

The following summer, Allen went in search of an inexpensive chassis—and found one from an SS 50, which was first completely disassembled. Logically, to fit the 98 into the chassis of an original SS 50, quite a bit of welding was required on the frame. "I had to cut quite a bit off the main beam of the backbone frame to accommodate the upright cylinder and especially the intake manifold," Allen explains. To be on the safe side and prevent frame breakage, two struts were welded in from the rear to the swing-arm pivot point. The battery, previously housed in the side of the frame, no longer had a place there. It disappeared into the rear apron of the homemade seat.

Allen's first SS 100 was assembled in the kitchen at home. It is street legal and suitable for everyday use. The cute "hump" at the rear of the seat was created from a cut-open headlight housing.

"This idea came to me only when no reasonable seat could be found." A BSA headlight cut in half was neatly fitted, and the engine first roughly plugged into the chassis in the kitchen after a homemade intake manifold connected the rear cylinder to the twenty-barrel Keihin carburetor. The pedals—the chassis of the 1975 SS 50 had to have pedals at the time—were removed and the footrest system of an earlier version was fitted. Originally, the Honda was equipped with disc brakes, but they were mechanically "over the Jordan" along with the caliper, so Allen resorted to a C 50 front wheel, which was installed upside down to attach the brake anchor plate to the standpipe. As for the exhaust system, Allen used what he had lying around.

The next spring, the Honda SS 100 was finally ready for its maiden voyage, which it completed with flying colors after some carburetor tuning. Since Allen had already set his sights on numerous new projects, the lightweight disappeared a short time later into the second floor of his home. From there, we recently took the little homebuilt 98 out for a test ride, which wasn't easy because the noble tinkerer had broken his arm in a motocross. Unfortunately, the 6-volt battery had weakened due to the long idle time, which later became noticeable by dropouts in the lower speed range.

Nevertheless, the engine didn't lose a drop of oil while we tortured the homebuilt model through the Berkshire countryside. With just under 9 hp, the Honda easily manages the 100 kph (62 mph) speed limit, since it is only a few kilograms heavier than the single-cylinder original. Allen has thus once again created a respectable one-off. It should be clear that this is not his last project—but it is undoubtedly one of the prettiest.

A MONKEY STREET FIGHTER

Can you make a streetfighter out of a tiny Honda Monkey? They have to look brutish, have a displacement of at least 1,000 cc, have ultrawide tires, and basically be completely illegal. It also works with 100 cc and small wheels; the Monkey pictured here is the best proof of that—when the pictures were shot, there had not been time for the TÜV (Technical Inspection Association) inspection and official blessing.

The bike's owner is a well-known face in the scene around small Hondas with the horizontal four-stroke engine—although here he is wearing a mask in honor of the great vehicle. Before he ran Mr. Monkey and Dr. Dax in Hanover, Germany, Nikolaus Tams was a self-employed industrial designer by profession and had been taking care of legendary Honda singles of all kinds since 1994. He has been "bitten by the Monkey" since his brother once gave him a ride on an S 90. He owned seventeen more Monkeys when the pictures were taken—and today there are sure to be even more in the Monkey stable in Hanover. Logically, many Takegawa parts are installed here: the frame, tank, lamp, and engine housing are the only original parts. The conversion was worth 23,000 marks more than two decades ago—but the rebuilt Z 50 J can still be seen (and heard) today.

Monkey Business: Behind the mask is Nikolaus Tams, an old master of the Honda 50/70 tuning scene. He knows the Japanese tuners and knows which components fit and are good.

DRIVE

Modified from 106 cc, power about 15 hp, Takegawa cylinder head, long-stroke crankshaft, and larger camshaft. Intake valve 23.8 mm, exhaust valve 20.8 mm diameter, reinforced valve springs, light alloy oil cooler, three-plate manual clutch on gearbox input shaft, five-speed gearbox, reinforced oil pump, 26 mm carburetor, Mikuni round slide valve, adapted engine ventilation with expansion tank, CDI ignition

ALL THE TRIMMINGS

Hydraulic telescopic fork, 27 mm standpipes, milled triple clamps with fork stabilizer, all-body swing arm extended by 160 mm, eccentric chain tensioner, disc brake with double piston caliper in front, disc with single piston caliper in rear, 8-inch rims, silver anodized, steering damper, retracted footrest system, reinforced sport suspension struts, megaphone exhaust by Dräger, single seat with rear spoiler

TOPPINGS

Takegawa speedometer up to 87 mph (140 kph), tachometer up to 14,000 rpm, oil thermometer

As you can see, Hartmut Merkle is someone who has special ideas and can also implement them.

DOUBLE FLEET

If you're seeing double here, you're seeing right (again); this Honda actually has two cylinders. True to the motto "There's no substitute for displacement, except more displacement," Hartmut Merkle from Aichtal, Germany, reached deep into his toolbox to implant a double heart into the Z 50 R from the 1980s. He, too, is an old hand in the Honda scene and knows how to rebuild a vehicle professionally and durably. Nevertheless, he turned a new cylinder head into scrap on the first milling attempt, but he didn't let that get him down. Three individual components had to be used to manufacture the crankshaft; it was clear to him in advance that the oil pump would have to be reinforced. One overhead camshaft per cylinder head came from the SS 50 parts store.

A suitable O-ring for sealing the cylinder heads in series was found in the accessories trade; the long output shaft was supplied by a Dutch Honda. To enlarge the oil circuit, the builder gave his Super Monkey a rebuilt oil cooler, which is the only component of German manufacture – from a BMW R 1100 GS! Is the Monkey street legal? It deserves to be! Because the noble tinkerer has invested about five hundred working hours, as well as about 7,000 marks into it. For those who are interested, Hartmut Merkle runs a motorcycle museum together with his brother. It is located 12.4 miles (20 kilometers) south of Stuttgart, on the B 27, in the town of Aichtal-Aich. For about twenty years, more than one hundred motorcycles have been on display on three floors, an area of about 4,844 square feet (450 square meters). There it stands: the Monkey Special, alongside other members of its family.

DRIVE

144 cc (2 × 72 cc), about 15 hp, compression ratio 12, two SS 50 camshafts, crankshaft made from individual components, four-speed gearbox, twin-disc oil bath clutch, two 20 mm round slide carburetors from Keihin, shortened intake manifolds, SS 50 contact-controlled ignition. Oil cooler from the BMW R 1100 GS adapted to fit.

CHASSIS

Hydraulic front fork, shortened Honda CB 50 swing arm, Brembo disc brakes with steel flex lines in front, chromed 8-inch rims

TOPPINGS

Daytona tachometer, Takegawa tach drive adapted on left cylinder, JMCA double exhaust

The two-cylinder Monkey was built years ago, but it doesn't look old-fashioned by a long shot. A suitable O-ring seals the two cylinder heads against one another; it was found in the aftermarket.

Quirky but well thought out: the twin still ignites mechanically via an interrupter; two 20 mm Keihins sit on shortened carburetor necks. A BMW GS donated the oil cooler.

13
10
Racing Team

SPORT ON SMALL HONDAS

MUDDY FUN IN THE MONKEY STABLE

Insiders have known it for a long time: contrary to popular belief, the "pit biking" that has emerged in recent years with the four-stroke engines familiar from the Monkey is not a trend sport from the US.

The sport was invented in the early 1970s in the "wild south" of Germany. There, in 1974, the first official "Monkeycross" event took place in Diegelsberg (district of Göppingen). Shortly thereafter, several clubs joined forces and founded the German Monkey Club (DMC) in 1976. The German Monkeycross Championship shows that four-stroke 50s and 125s in mini chassis on 12- and 10-inch lug tires—the legendary Honda Monkey and its replicas—can bounce spectacularly through the dust.

Yes, the event is the German championship, even though the starter and date lists show a clear preponderance of participants in the southwest of the country. The DMC has been organizing the Monkeycross races as a championship series under the auspices of the German Motorsport Association (DMV) for forty-seven years now.

In the early years, of course, the riders exclusively used Honda Monkey engines. The class division was even simpler; the youngest participants (eight to twelve years) drove original vehicles, the older ones performance-optimized prototypes with 50 or 75 cc engines. For the latter, only the engine, vehicle, and tire size were specified. Also in the running were sidecars in a separate class with 90 cc engines. Self-built vehicles dominated the scene—tuning produced around 15 hp at 14,000 rpm, and chassis conversions with manual clutches, five-speed transmissions, and long suspension travel were not unusual. Seven races were held per year, and the number of

HONDA

REDUCED TO THE BARE MINIMUM IN ORDER TO WIN: ALMOST NOTHING ORIGINAL IS LEFT ON THE MONKEY. BUT LONG SWING ARMS AND LONG SPRING TRAVEL ARE A MUST.

spectators increased to up to 1,500 per event. Tuned engines wore out quickly, and burst engines and transmission damage from hard use were not uncommon. Participants and sponsors quickly learned that the sport was not free—one of the reasons why there were fewer active Monkeycrossers in the mid-1980s. It was also not uncommon for permits to hold events to be denied due to more stringent laws. But since the revival of the scene through other four-stroke engines and a variety of now readily available vehicles such as CRF 50, Thumpstar, Motovert, PitPro, and company, the Monkeycross—like the DMC—has been given a breath of fresh air and has returned to its roots.

As before, the championship is held in several displacement and age classes, with the technical specifications and organizational details laid down in the DMC regulations. For example, all pit bikes must have the Monkey-typical four-stroke engine. At Monkeycross events, therefore, not only children and young people do their laps on the little machines, but adults as well. This results in enormous fun for the riders and is a special feast for the eyes for the spectators. The racing runs each last ten or fifteen minutes. In recent years, numerous female participants have also taken part in Monkeycross and are not to be underestimated. This success is due not only to the above-mentioned variety of models, but also to the class division made by the MSC (here: Monkeys and pit bikes with horizontal engines):

Class	Age	Vehicles
0	6–12	Monkeys / pit bikes up to 50 cc (max. 12-/10-inch wheels)
1	10 and up	Pit bikes up to 110 cc (max. 12-/14-inch wheels) and CRF-100 vehicles
2	12 and up	Monkeys / pit bikes up to 125 cc (max. 10-/12-inch wheels)
4	13 and up	Pit bikes up to 200 cc (max. 12-/14-inch wheels) and XR-200 vehicles

The Feuchtwangen, HMV Hepsisau, and RKV Kirchheim/Teck clubs organize events in Güntersleben, Feuchtwangen, Maitzborn, Kirchheim-Jesingen, and Weilheim. In 2017, for example, seventy-one participants competed in the six races.

Due to the local clubs involved in Monkeycross, the races are held mainly in southern Germany. Nevertheless, the events draw from an area that extends much farther. For example, riders come from Isny in Allgäu as well as from Cologne. And for some participants, the sport of Monkeycross has been a real career springboard. Martin Gölz and his codriver Ulli Rommel from Kirchheim/Teck are examples. Both started very early on riding modified Monkeys and won several German championship titles both in solo and team classes.

The DMC is represented online (www.facebook.com/monkeycross) and offers detailed information there.

BEING THERE IS EVERYTHING

It couldn't be easier: head to the dealer and load a minibike with a Monkey or an aftermarket engine or a budget Thumpstar onto the bus—the main thing is that it be air-cooled, have a 50 or 125 cc engine, and 12-/10-inch wheels—and you're in. According to the regulations, any Öhlins, Marzocchi, or cake fork can be screwed into the steering tube. A common feature of off-road use is the crisply short gear ratio. On most slopes, it's hardly possible to rev it up anyway. So be brave and go for the big sprocket! No larger than 10 inches. Supermoto brakes are not the order of the day here.

Of course, there are a few things to consider when tuning. The air-cooled single cylinder must remain as it is. Around it (i.e., mainly on the chassis), clever tinkerers, financially solid parts swappers, and thermodynamic tinkerers are allowed to let off steam—in keeping with the motto: Play without limits. Participant Axel Wendt, however, has built a water-cooled 125 cc top end from light metal on the CNC mill and optimized his engine with it. He invested 11,000 euros, as well as more than a complete day of pure cutting, and with it the single should now produce 25 hp. Although his work did not meet the regulations, he was still allowed to participate, though not competitively.

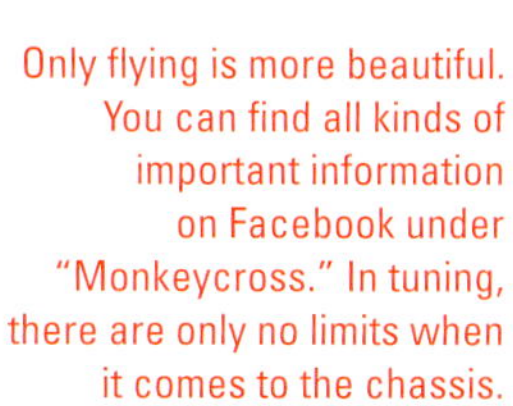

Everyone starts small. That's why there's Class 0.

Only flying is more beautiful. You can find all kinds of important information on Facebook under "Monkeycross." In tuning, there are only no limits when it comes to the chassis.

THE ROKKER
3

HORSEPOWER AND OPTICS

Whether on the track or at the Dutch Honda Day, fans of the Honda horizontal singles are not your usual motorcycle fans.

WHILE TWO OR THREE DECADES AGO, ALL FANS WERE GOING TO TUNED MATERIAL, TODAY THE TREND OFTEN GOES TO THE ORIGINAL. SOME SPECIALISTS MAKE THE BEST OF BOTH.

It's not just Sabine and fellow racer Jasmin who are having fun with the Dax-Manufaktur Racing team, the members of which are really letting it rip here at the Newchurch Club.

YOUNGSTERS FROM HAMBURG

Eight Honda Dax minibikes and three Monkeys are currently at Thomas Disch's Dax Manufaktur in Hamburg, Germany. Some vehicles have just been disassembled; others are waiting to receive their finishing touches. They should soon look like they're fresh off the assembly line—or even better.

The Hamburg native only knows what is in store for him once a vehicle has been unloaded and thoroughly checked. Think "hidden defects." Thomas has already had a few negative "highlights" in his workshop and has a small cabinet of horrors in his photo and workshop archive. These include a steering-head nut that had been "fixed" to the steering tube with countless layers of electrical tape. "I discovered this when I wanted to retighten the steering head," Thomas remembers. "Fortunately, only the nut thread was gone; the rest was still usable." Some of the other horrors have included a rear chain sprocket whose thirty-eight teeth were as sharp as razor blades, and a throttle valve that had been sawed off so short that the clip for holding the needle barely fit in. And almost daily, there are other surprises for Thomas. "Recently there was a vehicle that had the needle clip completely missing," he says. "The previous owner had taken a piece of wire and wrapped it around the jet needle. It actually held. And the engine ran."

Thomas Disch quit his job as an advertising specialist back in 2016—and his side hustle turned into a full-time job. Up to ten complete Dax or Monkey restorations emerge between late fall and the start of the season. Thanks to the move to a new, more spacious workshop in Hamburg's Winterhude district, productivity has increased even more. "Around 30 square meters [323 square feet] of showroom and office, a nice warehouse, and almost 100 square meters [1,076 square feet] of workshop space," explains the trained businessman. "You can work with that." Dax-Manufaktur Hamburg's first residence was the cellar of Disch's home, after which he moved to a room on the first floor of a former air raid shelter in Gertigstraße.

Thomas's most spectacular order was from a group of buyers that wanted six Daxes made to the same specification—but each of the future owners had their own ideas about the paint job. "The delivery to Sylt was quite a colorful event," Thomas recalls.

Three years ago, he also launched his Dax-Manufaktur Racing Team, which has already managed to take third place in the open 8-liter class at the annual Newchurch Club event in Austria. The duo of Sabine Singenberger and Jasmin Fuchs from Zurich is fast on the road—because it's fun and, of course, also because their machine has it all. Based on a CT 70, vintage 1971, the racing Dax owned by the two Swiss women has around five times as much horsepower as the original. This was made possible by a complete drive system from tuning supplier Takegawa. "It's been going strong for two years now, after the chassis was also significantly improved," explains Thomas. On the steering tube, there's now a pair of shortened upside-down fork stems from the Honda MSX in specially adapted triple clamps. To ensure that the 125 cc factory engine gets the horses safely onto the road, the rear shock absorbers have been replaced by fully adjustable gas-pressure racing specimens.

The store is humming; current lead time is six months. "Little things like changing Bowden cables are sometimes in between. But meeting the agreed deadlines for customizing and restoration projects has top priority," Thomas says. If a part is not in stock or repairable, a call to a dealer or colleague is often all that is needed. Thomas Disch is well connected (not least thanks to his many years of experience in advertising), including to friendly dealers and service providers.

In Hamburg-Winterhude, barn finds or neglected Dax minibikes are rebuilt like new or entirely to customer specifications.

The Dax-Manufaktur Racing Team is also very busy between races. The riders from Zurich rely on the Hamburg-based mechanic, who has tickled well over 20 hp out of the original CT 70.

BACK IN BLACK
DAX
MANUFAKTUR
FUCHS
BACK IN BLACK
HONDA

LIKE THESE TWO YOUNG WOMEN, MANY HONDA RACERS ARE SEEN ONLY FROM BEHIND. THANKS TO TAKEGAWA, MSX, AND CHASSIS COMPONENTS FROM RACING SPORT, THIS RACING DAX IS ALWAYS COMPETITIVE.

"ONE MUST WORK HARD TO BREAK A VEHICLE LIKE THIS"

Thomas Disch discusses his career as a Dax and Monkey specialist and his experiences in the care and use of the little Honda, which can handle a lot—but not everything.

Thomas, when and how did you actually get to know the species you have lying around here, complete and in parts? Was it because you are a nostalgic person, or rather because you needed something to ride during your school days?
Well, during my school days, here in Hamburg, I always thought the little things with the throaty four-stroke sound were cooler than the two-stroke scooters. Back then, 40 kph [24.8 mph] was still the order of the day; now, Mokicks are allowed to go 45 [28 mph]. However, I didn't have a Dax or Monkey myself back then, because I was feverishly saving up for my driver's license and my first car.

Small vehicles have always had a magical attraction for you?
There's no denying that. It was no coincidence that even before I had my driver's license in my pocket, I was enthusiastic about an Austin Mini and not a Scirocco or a Kadett. By the way, many of my customers actually have an affinity for the old English Mini as well.

Your first little Honda—when did it come into the house?
When I was thirty, my old sandbox buddy suddenly appeared in my front yard with a Dax, saying, "Look at this; I just bought it." I was blown away, and the very next weekend I was browsing through an ad in Hamburg (the online platforms we know today didn't exist at the time) and immediately found a Dax built in 1988. I drove straight to the old man and bought his sweetheart from him. I still own and drive this Dax today.

When did you start with the optical and technical tuning?
That came gradually; through contacts I got to know what is officially feasible. As a result of tinkering with my moped, I had accumulated all kinds of parts, which I then used for the first commissioned work: a CT 70 with a 125 cc engine for a good friend. He then recommended me to others in his circle of friends, and so the whole thing developed a certain momentum. With my knowledge of marketing and advertising, it was relatively easy to give the trade, which was founded in 2012, a bit of a boost. After all, a small website and a bit of social media are mandatory these days. And a little bit of racing provides the exciting content to go with it.

Restored with passion and intellect: Thomas Disch has been restoring Dax and Monkey minibikes of all kinds full-time since 2016.

What is particularly important in the care of Dax and Monkey? Are they tasks that are obvious?

Most of them are: oil level, changing the oil, and valve adjustment—or put simply, a regular inspection is obvious and necessary. It's the greasy jobs that are usually forgotten (or deliberately avoided): cleaning the oil centrifuge in the clutch body or maintaining the famous "rattle fork." Unfortunately, things like this quickly lead to greatly increased wear and not infrequently to defective parts. All the more dramatic when it comes to parts that are almost impossible to obtain today.

Is it possible to restore a Dax or Monkey to completely original condition?

Yes, it is still possible to almost 100 percent. When I restore such a moped, then I really do everything: disassemble the moped and check the condition of all its components. All painted parts are chemically stripped, blasted if necessary, and then repainted by a specialist—if desired, of course, in the usual "candy" tones used by Honda at the time. Each engine is disassembled down to the last bolt, cleaned, and checked for wear, with defective or suspect parts replaced and housing parts glass-bead-blasted. And then everything is neatly put back together. Finally, everything is reassembled using original spare parts. Only for very few parts does one have to resort to (fortunately reasonable) repro parts. And a few technical details, such as a modern 12-volt electrical system and contactless ignition, can be added at the same time with little effort. If you then stick to a few rules, you really can't break such a little gem.

For more information:
info@dax-manufaktur.de
www.dax-manufaktur.de
www.facebook.com/daxmanufakturr

IMITATION IS THE SINCEREST FORM OF FLATTERY

A wide variety of imitations are on the market—and, yes, the quality of the imitations varies.

AFTER IMPORTATION OF THE DAX AND MONKEY STOPPED, RESOURCEFUL IMPORTERS RIGHTLY SENSED BUSINESS OPPORTUNITIES AND MARKET SHARES AND BEGAN MARKETING CHINESE VEHICLES. THERE WERE ALSO TECHNICAL IMPROVEMENTS. BUT THE CONCEPT OF THE SUPER CUB WAS ALSO COPIED IN ASIA AND SOMETIMES WAS MODIFIED WITH STRANGE DESIGN IDEAS.

For a number of years, the Chinese manufacturer Lifan also produced replicas of the ST 50 and the Z 50 J. As a modern addition, they have an electric starter, 12-volt electrical system, CDI ignition, and front disc brake.

A trade-show smash hit: Sachs's idiosyncratic MadAss made its debut at INTERMOT in September 2003, but it wasn't free of teething troubles either.

DAX REPRODUCTIONS

Fifteen years ago, manufacturer Skyteam started with the ST 110. With 6.7 hp, this replica of the ST 70 was barely faster than the original.

At the end of the 1990s, the importer drew a line under the revised Dax and halted imports. A little later, in 1999, production was finally discontinued. Patent protection also expired. The Chinese manufacturer Jincheng acquired the rights to the design for both the Dax and the Z 50 J and all other Monkey variants. Replicas soon appeared in many European countries. In Germany, it was Wolfgang Bern of Marburg with his Quickfoot that split the scene into original and replica fans. By the way, Bern started to produce the Quickfoot himself in 2004 with his own type approval, which was undoubtedly a good idea in terms of quality but certainly made the product itself more expensive, so that production was finally discontinued in 2007. But approximately 10,000 units were built—many of which certainly ended up attached to numerous motor homes.

Despite the sale of the manufacturing rights, Honda had reserved the right to reissue a small series of these vehicles per year. One can also assume that the demand for parts was so enormous that it was easily able to reduce inventories in this way and sell these vehicles to collectors as "special editions."

From 2005 onward, an ST replica was also available in the shape of the Skyteam ST 110. Importers were not exactly happy in the beginning; corrosion protection and paint quality were not what one was used to from the original. But they must have learned quickly—and even offered a larger fuel tank as a real improvement. Although the original Honda was economical, it had the same small 2.5-liter (0.66 gallon) tank as the ST 50 or ST 70, which required a visit to the gas station at least every 62 miles (100 km), as well as making the rider sweat at the pump over whether the minimum purchase of 2 liters would actually fit in the tank under the seat. The ST 110 could now accommodate 5.5 liters (1.45 gallons) of fuel, which was outwardly also due to modifications and reinforcements made to the frame.

Particularly in the case of the replicas that are still being sold—even as electric variants, by the way—it can often be seen that they have been "originalized" by some owners (e.g., with the classic Honda "mustache trainer" on the frame or the chrome-plated original exhaust). Often with conversions, it is possible to discover the original on which the custom bike was based only upon closer examination. In the US, approval guidelines are now quite different, so the replicas, as successful as they were in Europe, were often not so easy to get on the road there. But especially in the US, aftermarket parts, as well as entire aftermarket engines, are quite trendy. In Europe, original condition is more the order of the day. The fad for maximum displacement has now given way to more of a quality mindset at Dax and Monkey. Therefore, many unfinished or poor rebuilds are indeed offered for sale, while Honda barn finds are often rebuilt by professionals. The vast majority of the original spare parts are still available, albeit at prices that far exceed those made by the Chinese.

I was allowed to write a comparative satire of the "old" ST 70 against the replica in 2005 (*see box on opposite page*). In it, the two Minichamps meet and compete against each other in Shanghai. "Is the ST 110 a match for the Japanese original?" I asked—and chased the two minibikes through the urban jungle.

The electric starter of Estee Eleven-O, a Dax replica youngster, buzzed briefly, and the gearshift quickly clicked four times. After seeing a movie – Estee's favorite classic was playing – she saw the older lady standing at the side of the street. The headlight sparked suspiciously after 6 volts, the four-stroke ticking with too much valve clearance. "Do you know how I can get to Ma-Ni-Tou, the Tu-Ning grand master, as soon as possible?" asks the Dax.

"Sure," replies Miss Skyteam. "Just follow me. By the way, you remind me of Grandma. She was from Japan and wore a mustache trainer around her frame tube too."

Immediately, the two four-stroke engines begin bubbling away – Estee's a bit more aggressively, the faded oldie's more cautiously – and they weave their way through Shanghai's avalanches of cars. Estee tugs on the disc brake, briefly glances in the mirror, which unfortunately is vibrating violently as always, and turns off, followed by the red Honda, in the direction of the red-light district. All kinds of gangs roam around here – the Magic Monkeys, for example, who have recently been engaged in nasty burnout contests with the Lifan Tigers. Yesterday, their leader Maotse-Wum got it; he was found on the side of the road without a carburetor and with his 8-inch tires knifed off.

"A quick drink?" Estee asks the older Japanese vehicle. "Something to suck on would be great; after all, I'm almost on reserve," she explains. And after quickly unfolding the seat, she begins to look at the fuel level while her counterpart is still busy unlocking. Finally, she can take a closer look at it. The older lady, she thinks, is poorly off: she has no main stand, starts only with a kick, and still has an old-fashioned drum brake at the front, babbling about "innovative semiautomatics." She does not have a proper clutch. "Inherited from my great-grandmother, the Honda Super Cub." Nevertheless, her movements are controlled, she never seems overworked, and – despite her twenty-five years – has neither wrinkles nor rust. "That's how I want to look in twenty-five years," the bright red Chinese youngster thinks.

With a full tank of gas, the two leave the Fu Man Chu, Estee's favorite bar. After a few attempts at takeoff, Estee Seven-O must already be a little tipsy, because her machine won't run again until the fifth kick. Then the duo roars on toward the finish. Hiccups manifest themselves in all kinds of wheelies on Estee's part, while the Japanese seems in high spirits. "Phew, I'm breaking a sweat," she says, flipping down both halves of her handlebars in high spirits.

When they arrive at the Grand Master's, they are met by two trainers and immediately race around another course. In the race, the old lady has a hard time with her semiautomatic. The first of the three gears is on top; neutral has to be skipped with a double shift, and that takes time. A wellness program? "Just the right thing for me," says Miss Seven-O. Especially when she sees the measurement result. "Oh, 59 mph? I did over 70 once." Miss Eleven-O takes a more relaxed view. "I'm going to move – to Germany. There are great jobs for us there. How about it – are you coming?"

I came to the following conclusion at the time: "Dax vobiscum (Dax be with you). Well-maintained original Daxes rise steadily in price and last forever, but the driving performance of the fun bike is less than exhilarating. It gets along much easier in everyday traffic with a four-speed transmission and electric starter."

In fact, with current Dax replicas, registrations and modifications are easier than with "old" vehicles – such as 160 cc engines (not least thanks to the frame reinforcements) and tubeless 100/90-10 tires. As active dealers confirm, fuel pumps have been standard for three years, and thanks to three-phase alternators, night riding has become safer.

X-lite
Super
SPORTS
Super

Even at trade fairs, Cub variants could always be seen at INTERMOT and EICMA booths until 2016. Since Euro 4 came into force, there have been few 125 cc newcomers of this type.

EVEN BEFORE HONDA CAME OUT WITH THE INNOVA 125 AND THE C 125 SUPER CUB, THERE WERE ATTEMPTS BY CHINESE MANUFACTURERS SUCH AS ZONGSHEN TO ESTABLISH MODERN CUB COPIES IN THE EUROPEAN UNION LIGHT-MOTORCYCLE MARKET.

The Kymco Nexxon: this well-made copy was also short lived but is a possible everyday alternative for little money.

The descendant of the rather conservative ZS 50 3 was trimmed to an Asian racing look, and it was therefore only a moderate sales success in Europe.

SUPER CUB REPRODUCTIONS: MODERN VS. CLASSIC VERSIONS

While the former Honda licensee Kymco was late in launching its Nexxon 50 big-bike variant on the fiercely competitive 28 mph (45 kph) market, and only for a short time, the German Zongshen importer was faster. After a 50 cc variant, the Chinese-built NEXT GENERATION entered the market in the mid-2000s, advertised as "the fuel-saving sports bike."

"We can take away the agonizing decision between sportiness and low fuel consumption: the CAB 125 NEXT GENERATION is very frugal and yet a zippy vehicle. It is not just its sporty appearance that makes this scooter an eye-catcher; its technology is also impressive! The ergonomically designed instrument console and the advantage of being able to sit comfortably and upright are also convincing." This was the lead text for the Zongshen in the German brochure.

CAB 125 NEXT GENERATION—Specifications

Engine

Displacement/stroke .... 125 cc / 4-stroke
Output KW/HP .... 6.2 kW / 8.43 hp
Maximum speed .... 49.7 mph (80 kph)
Transmission .... 4-speed semiautomatic

Fuel

Tank capacity .... 3.5 liters (0.9 gallons)

Brakes

Front/rear .... disc/disc

Dimensions

Seat height .... 29.9 inches (760 mm)
Weight (empty) .... 212 pounds (96 kg)

Annual production by the manufacturer, which was only founded in 1992, was already 3.5 million vehicles fifteen years ago, and there was a cooperation agreement with Piaggio and a collaboration with Harley-Davidson. In 2006, I was allowed to ride the first 125, whose design certainly went down well in Asia but didn't exactly appeal to a wide range of buyers in Germany.

A BIT OF BOTH

What is it: scooter or motorcycle? The answer is, simply, a bit of both. Vacationers in the Far East are familiar with the countless four-stroke mopeds with leg shields and low step-throughs that whizz around Asia, all of them offshoots of the ancestor that Soichiro Honda introduced back in 1958. Many manufacturers have copied the million-dollar thing or still produce it; every Chinese motorcycle factory has one or more bootlegs of it in its program. Here in Germany, the unpretentious Honda 50 Super Cub had no chance against Kreidler, Zündapp, and Company in the 1960s, so a larger-displacement version was never offered. But today, importer Fritz Röth, who also offers a mokick version, hopes that a modern copy of the four-stroke economy motorcycle could once again have a chance on the market. His Asian bread-and-butter machines are made by Zongshen, currently China's best-known manufacturer, and recently even a contractual partner of Piaggio and Harley-Davidson. The horizontal OHC engine of the Cab 125 starts either with a kick or the push of a button. It is still equipped with a carburetor and sounds throaty; the gear selection is semiautomatic by foot shift lever, and neutral is at the top. A step on the gearshift lever opens the centrifugal clutch – also following the foolproof Honda model – mechanically when changing gears. If it is properly adjusted, those with Honda Dax and Monkey experience can use it almost like a conventional manual clutch. On the Cab 125, this works almost better than on the original, because the four-plate clutch does not operate on the crankshaft but on a low-wear intermediate shaft located behind it. Thanks to 17-inch wheels and motorcycle-like weight distribution, the Asian model rides accurately and easily, even if the suspension elements are only moderately responsive and have a slack design. The chain is, as with the Honda original, fortunately fully encapsulated, and the side stand's simple reset mechanism has no ignition breaker. The disc brakes, with double piston calipers, function acceptably but without a perceptible pressure point; a short cable activates the brake pump mounted next to the rear wheel. The high-torque power plant is not free of vibrations, but it consumes pleasantly little. One tankful of fuel from the 3.5-liter tank under the lockable but uncomfortably stepped seat is enough for the Cab 125 to cover more than 150 kilometers (93 miles). Inexperienced riders should always keep an eye on the gear indicator integrated in the cockpit, because the gearshift works according to the rotation principle. If you continue pedaling after fourth gear, you end up in neutral again, and the next foot movement is followed by first gear again, which could have serious consequences under certain circumstances.

Starting in 2006, a ZS 125 was also available in Germany from the manufacturer Zongshen. Importer Zweirad Röth did not find many customers at that time.

Minimalism meets zeitgeist: the Sachs MadAss was also available as a 125 cc version, but the niche was too small even for the Nuremberg manufacturer.

EASTERN EUROPEAN MARKETS

A "special edition" of the Jawa Pionyr retro limited to five hundred vehicles should not go unmentioned. Much cheaper was the Jawa Betka, an interesting mix of Honda Camino chassis and four-speed Cub replica unit. Thanks to a dealer network, there are still numerous Romet Ogar machines on the road in spite of Euro 4. Thanks to suspension strut sleeves, drum brakes, headlights, and taillights, they bear a strong resemblance to the CD 50 classics. The only visually disturbing elements are the attachments for exhaust gas recirculation, which are of course also mounted on newer Dax and Monkey replicas with carburetors. The new fuel-injected models with 125 cc engines appear tidier again.

Many of the Zongshen 125s were not sold, and customers who were patient for a few more years could acquire either a Honda ANF 125 or Innova—or a classic SMC variant with short swing arm and drum brakes, available for sale mostly via the Netherlands and from 2011 to 2016 also from German dealers. For example, by Stefan Berthold of Nuremberg, who last year sold several variants: the 50 as a three-speed, a 107 cc, and even a 120 cc as a "Kellerharrer Cub" with daily registration and direct import. However, the Cub replicas produced by Chongqing in Guangyu were reworked and re-tired by the Dutch importer, making it look confusingly similar to the C 90 with round lights. A completely new design concept for the use of the horizontal single-cylinder, four-stroke engine was developed at Sachs in Nuremberg, Germany. The MadAss with tubular frame offered futuristic minimalism but displayed some (design) weaknesses in everyday use.

The Romet Ogar is an Asian vehicle, but it will still be manufactured with fuel injection at the end of 2020 and is homologated for the Polish manufacturer.

The Chinese four-stroke engine fits perfectly into the slim lines of the Jawa Pionyr. The Jawa Pionyr retro was available as a 50 cc as well as a limited-edition 125 cc (*below*).

Jawa Betka: Also an oddball mix of Honda Camino styling paired with a conventionally coupled Jincheng four-stroke engine.

From the carbureted version to the fuel-injected version, Skyteam has made the leap to Euro 4 and, with the larger 5.5 liter (1.45 gallon) tank, has also improved the range of the classic replica.

Pedicure: the Quickfoot was introduced by Marburg-based Open Concepts maker Wolfgang Bern twenty years ago.

THE QUICKFOOT WILL SOON BE ELECTRIC

Around twenty years ago, Wolfgang Bern launched the Quickfoot as a replica of the classic Z 50 J. Then, the machine still used mature four-stroke engine technology, but a new electrically powered successor is soon to appear, built by the Hanseatische Fahrzeug Manufaktur GmbH. Bern promises solid German workmanship as well as carefree riding fun, thanks to various engine versions, from a moped to a 19 kw / 25 hp motorcycle version. All frame parts are milled from aircraft aluminum, satin-glass-bead-blasted, and anodized to a high standard. Modern LED technology provides bright light and a safe ride. The 10-inch aluminum alloy wheels are designed to give the classic-trimmed newcomer a retro look, along with a comfortable café racer-style seat. Modern meets traditional, which is why the vehicle has a CAN bus and Bluetooth connectivity to the owner's cell phone. Many vehicle functions and information are then also available to the driver on the Quickfoot app. A dealer network provides tuning and accessories and handles inspections. Future Quickfoot owners will receive personal support from the manufacturer in word and deed.

It's not for children or Tama Tech use. The vehicle dimensions should not hide the fact that the Quickfoot is a motorcycle that requires a driver's license, and in the most powerful variant, it is even supposed to get down to business with 25.5 hp.

Mokick and light-motorcycle versions of the Quickfoot were available. Toward the end of the 2000s decade, the Quickfoot was also manufactured and rehomologated in Germany. An electric version is under development.

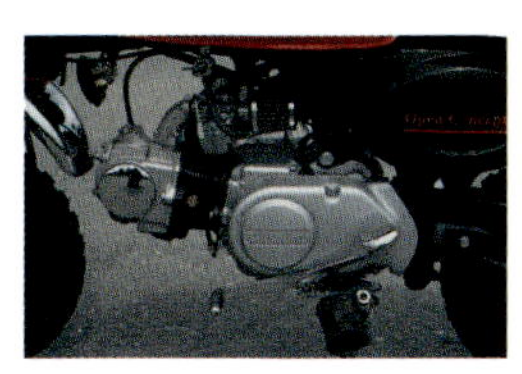

HONDA
TRAIL 70
JADE-H

BUYING AND SELLING

What, where, and how: Disassembled mass-produced bearings, as shown here in the picture, are now rare. Restored vehicles are expensive but often cheaper than the DIY version.

DEALERS SPECIALIZING IN SMALL HONDAS CANNOT BE FOUND ON EVERY STREET CORNER. HOWEVER, THERE ARE MANY INTERESTING WORKSHOPS, WHICH DO NOT LIMIT THEMSELVES TO DEALING WITH THE DAX AND MONKEY. IN GENERAL, YOU CAN STILL FIND A LOT OF INTERESTING THINGS AT OLD-TIMER MARKETS—IF YOU LIKE TO RUMMAGE.

Barn party: Kjell's lavish showroom is located on the second floor.

The Utrecht-based company has since translated its Dutch name; Fourstroke-barn just sounds more international.

There are still plenty of used Super Cubs to be found in Japan. Kjell's employees collect together deals for him in Japan and fill the containers.

FOURSTROKEBARN IN UTRECHT:

MIXED TRADE

For lovers of Honda's four-stroke models, Kjell van Oostrum's workshop is both a barn party and a showroom. In addition to Dax, Monkey, and Super Cub variants, the Dutchman imports and repairs single-cylinder exotics, including the mopeds that rolled off the Honda assembly line in Aalst in the 1960s.

It's half past nine in the industrial area of Maarsen, near Utrecht in the Netherlands. It is autumn, crisp but sunny. The two rolling shutter gates along the Maarsenbroeksedijk on the busy Amsterdam-Rhine canal have long since been raised, revealing the five large, world-famous letters in capitals: HONDA. Engines lie next to a lavish workbench, and tanks and flashing chrome ornaments are draped in several display cases. Right next to them, the Honda company's founder, Soichiro Honda, smiles at the visitor in a remarkably large portrait. In the middle of the shelves full of spare parts, a good-humored bearded man is squeezing through. "You are in luck, Wib," Kjell replies to his counterpart on the cell phone. He had briefly checked on the shelf to make sure that the caller was not making the trip to see him in vain. Wib, as we are about to learn, is a retiree but still rides his C 50 DX almost every day. "He maintains the bright red thing, which looks like it just rolled off the assembly line, only the speedometer probably doesn't work right now," Kjell explains.

But it's not just actuating cables and speedometer shafts that the owner of the Fourstrokebarn seems to be well stocked with. "I also have all kinds of things in stock for vehicles from the '90s," the thirty-two-year-old proudly explains as he prepares a vehicle for another customer who has announced his arrival on this Friday morning. The forest-green Motra 50 is an odd, little-known four-stroke Honda, a kind of mix between off-road minibike and military motorcycle. Like many of the two hundred or so vehicles waiting here for enthusiasts, the Motra comes directly from Japan. Just a few days ago, another container arrived from Asia via Rotterdam, containing around fifty used enthusiast vehicles, all Hondas. "These are all 50, 70, and 90 cc machines, of course with proper export papers so that they can be registered in the EU. To make the container worthwhile, all kinds of spare parts are added: things that are otherwise only available – if at all – from wholesalers for big money. In my case, secondhand but affordable," explains the importer.

Sheet metal, steel, plastic, or electrics: if you are looking for parts, you will often find what you are looking for in Utrecht—rarely new, but usable and cheap.

UNUSUAL MINIATURES

The bestselling single-cylinder machines in the Netherlands are predominantly Dax, Monkey, and sporty SS 50 copies, but also virtually unknown 17-inch models such as the Honda CD Benly, Solo, and Jazz as well as variants of the Ape 50, next to newer and old Super Cubs, which the red-haired Kjell has imported for several years. And not without success, admittedly, because the demand for such little-known exotics has grown enormously. Many a collector's vehicle, for which German collectors search like a needle in a haystack, can still be found in the Netherlands far more effortlessly, since those in the bicycle nation continue happily and more frequently to ride the *fiets* (bicycles) and *bromfiets* (mopeds) of their youth, instead of consigning them to their garages as dust catchers. Kjell knows this and has adapted to it; his business no longer bears the original Dutch name Viertaktschuur but has been renamed the English equivalent for international customers. "In 2009, I started my store as the Viertaktschuur, initially quite modestly in my parents' house. It went better and better as a part-time job, until in 2015 I was able to rent here on the edge of the industrial area. First of all, I finished a hall, which was soon bursting at the seams. In 2017, the second hall was also finished, and now I could almost use a third," explains the trained welder.

The layout is well thought out and well structured. While current customer vehicles and restoration projects are stored on the first floor and can thus be quickly jacked up and disassembled on the lifting platform in the spacious work area at the rear, parts of Honda vehicles and also all other 50, 70, and 90 cc engines (such as usable drive components) are neatly arranged by number on shelves and await customers. Around ten Honda Ape and Honda CD Benly vehicles are stored together with chassis parts in a separate room on the second floor. Right next to it, we enter Kjell's actual "showroom," in which all his recently arrived vehicles are carefully lined up in a row. Just behind, a single flight of stairs farther on, we find ourselves in the small room—spotless and with a white paper background, opposite which stands a tripod. Here, the "barn owner" carefully photographs all the vehicles and parts. "My brother Bjorn helps me with the website, where all the vehicles and many parts can be seen and described. With zoom, of course, so you can see details as well. Well-lit photos are half the battle and show people what to expect," explains the Dutchman.

Fourstrokebarn also has special variants in its portfolio, such as the Little Cub on 14-inch wheels or the Press Cub, equipped with more powerful brakes, extra luggage rack, and special headlights.

MADE IN AALST

"Honda's status was different in Belgium and Holland, but also in Luxembourg and to some extent in parts of Switzerland, than it was in Germany," says Kjell's long-time friend Robin, who has come out of the office for a coffee and admits that he was curious to see what was unpacked from the shipping container. In May 1963, Honda opened its first plant in Europe in the Belgian town of Aalst—the company founder had cleverly chosen a structurally weak area and invested the equivalent of around two million euros in order to receive the same or similar treatment as domestic manufacturers in terms of tax and customs law within what was then still called the EEC. In addition to the C 100, the approximately two hundred workers produced special mopeds for the teens of the time in accordance with Dutch and Belgian pedal regulations. The C 310, developed from the C 240, a simpler version of the Super Cub then available in Japan with an OHV engine, looked strikingly similar to the Zündapp Combinette, at least from a distance. A few years later, this was followed by a sporty counterpart, the C 320, and then the TT 50. In 1966, the P50 moped with a four-stroke engine in the rear wheel, which was also offered here for a short time, was added, soon to be replaced for girls by the likewise four-stroke Amigo and Novio models, then by sportier 24.8 mph (40 kph) versions called the PS and PC 50. In parallel, the Dax and Monkey were imported into Belgium, the Netherlands, and Luxembourg in the 1970s, but far more popular forty years ago was the SS 50, which is also highly prized by Kjell's customers. "As a rule, the pedals, which were required by law in Holland, were removed and replaced by footrests and kick-starters," Robin states. "The English had the same problem from 1974 on—mopeds designated as 30 mph had to have pedals for a few years, and it wasn't until the mid-'80s that this requirement came to an end again."

Two-wheeler production in Aalst came to an end in 1995, after the workforce had already been "healthily reduced" from 213 to 98 workers ten years earlier. The four-stroke Honda had already been replaced by two-stroke models for the moped clientele by the end of the 1970s. The Camino and the Wallaroo were the last Honda 50s to roll off the assembly lines, which by then had already been largely converted to car parts.

Even today, the Little Cub as well as the Standard Cub are produced as 50 cc variants—with Honda PGM FI fuel injection and according to Japanese registration requirements.

If you want to restore a C 240 Port Cub, you need patience and good contacts in Asia. A C 310 is much easier, since it was sold in Belgium, the Netherlands, and Luxembourg.

EXPLORING THE INVENTORY

It's lunchtime; time for a snack. Michiel, who has his two Honda Chalys across the street, brings along a batch of burgers. "He's constantly working on the green CF at the moment," Kjell explains. "But the yellow one is running great." According to the owner, a good one hundred hours of work has gone into the 140 cc CF; the Chinese Lifan engine produces 9 hp and has a 24 mm carburetor. "Every now and then, it gives me trouble," says Michiel, armed with a screwdriver. So a test ride is imminent.

Robin also wants to know how the white CD 50 Benly runs. OK, explains the workshop owner, who has just been working on the electrics of the angular Motra. Wib also joins in, curious to see if the shaft actually reactivates the speedometer. The party interested in the Motra shows up, and the green Japanese bike changes hands a short time later. "I don't have to put them on the Net; only about 3,000 of them were built. It's a sure-fire success—even in Japan it was about twice as expensive as a Cub," says Kjell.

Next to it stands a blue one. The Press Cub is a workhorse, battered in Japan, with auxiliary headlight up front in case a full basket over the front wheel blocks the main headlight. Does it still run? The speedometer shows over 50,000 km (31,068 miles). The test lap impresses me; the 50 cc OHC engine chugs along barely audibly, and it shifts precisely and brakes properly. Honda quality, says the man in red. Chinese replicas, even parts of them, are a "no-go" for him. The price, Kjell? Not cheap, but reasonable. The name says it all, he says. Cheap urban, that is.

For more information:
www.fourstrokebarn.com

Kjell always has quite a few C 50s of all vintages for sale, such as this Press Cub. Besides their sturdy front rack and additional headlights, the blue transport versions have also reinforced axles and larger brake drums.

Stefan Berthold has already equipped one of his Cub imports to serve as a long-distance travel vehicle years ago. His Press Cub has a 50 kph (31 mph) registration and optionally also has a registered twin seat.

Whether original Little Cub or replica from China, the small Nuremberg workshop can help customers who have or are looking for such vehicles. Patience is an advantage here, because delivery from Asia can take a long time.

CUBS IN NUREMBERG

Stefan Berthold is a Cub expert from the German region of Franconia. As a former employee of the Honda dealership Motor Seidl, Stefan knows the Dax and Monkey but also the Super Cub and its inner workings very well. He has been a mechanic for twenty-two years and started his own business about six years ago after extensive experience in workshop and business management. He works together with an apprentice at Neubleiche 8 in downtown Nuremberg. He has already imported all kinds of Cubs from Japan, including the 100 cc replicas from China that came to Europe in containers via the Netherlands for a few years before the Euro 4 standard finally plugged this loophole as well. Anyone on the Honda Innova Forum knows the Franconian, who also often knows where the shoe pinches when it comes to Cub problems. "The importation of a Super Cub and the registration are, of course, always possible." The sticking point, naturally, is the cost, because until the millennium the Japanese—at least with the 50s, whether Super Cub, Little Cub, Press Cub, or Solo—had nothing to do with European markets. Exhaust emission certificates for vehicles of more recent vintage are possible but cost about 1,000 euros. Therefore, it often makes more sense to get a vehicle first registered prior to 1989—which, of course, has to be proven. From time to time, Stefan gets vehicles from Japan, which are then overhauled—exactly what this involves can be read about in the Honda Innova Forum.

Stefan had around thirty Cubs: originals and SMC replicas from China, which were available in 50 and 100 cc versions, on the workbench as well as in the showroom. Cabaret artist Jürgen Becker picked one up in Nuremberg the year before last. Stefan is proud not only of his black custom Cub, but also of his specially built "Traveler Cub" for long-distance riding. Based on a Press Cub, Stefan first disassembled the engine in great detail and rebuilt it—including new crankshaft bearings and

The auxiliary tank is located in the step-through, next to which there is a USB port and a 12-volt onboard power socket, oil canister, and tool bag. The light-alloy box, a protective grille with GPS holder, and the front and side pockets are also practical features.

Completely overhauled: the engine received a new crankshaft, crankshaft and gearbox bearings, pistons, and cylinders.

exact balancing of the shaft. "On the small touring machine, everything had to look good and be usable. Among other things, I made a fork mount for a Fuel Friend gas can and also mounted an auxiliary tank with its own bracket." For the adventurous look, a headlight grille was added at the top and bottom, as well as a mounting option for a GPS; an onboard power supply and USB sockets were also not forgotten.

He still owns his Traveler Cub, part of whose engine overhaul can also be read about on the Honda Innova Forum. "It's good for many, many miles—thanks in part to the special Press Cub parts that make the regular Super Cub an even tougher beast of burden, with special main and side stands, different, thicker axles, and larger brakes." By the way, this is not a joke and has been officially confirmed by Honda; plans were also in place for a 50 cc Press Cub to be manufactured in 2020 at the Kumamoto site for the Japanese market—in addition to the C 125 variants with Euro 4 for the European market. Since 2016, however, the 50 cc has no longer rolled off the line as a carbureted variant, but with Honda's PGM-FI (programmed fuel injection). "Another word about the Little Cub," explains Stefan, who had a silver-gray example of the typical girl's Cub in the workshop. "You just can't get new tires for it here—because it has 2.50-14 inch wheels—a size that is not put on any other vehicle in this country. Those are things to think about if it's going to be something special to drive."

For more information:
www.kellerharrer.de

HONDA
HONDA
MOTRA

ODD BIRDS

A very rare representative on the road: the Honda Motra was officially available only in Japan.

ALONG WITH ALL SPECIAL VERSIONS AND SPECIAL BIKES FOR CERTAIN TARGET GROUPS OR AGE GROUPS, THE C 100 HAS ALSO GIVEN RISE TO VEHICLES THAT CANNOT BE PIGEONHOLED AND ARE EXTREMELY RARE. HERE IS A SELECTION.

HONDA
S-110 DE LUXE

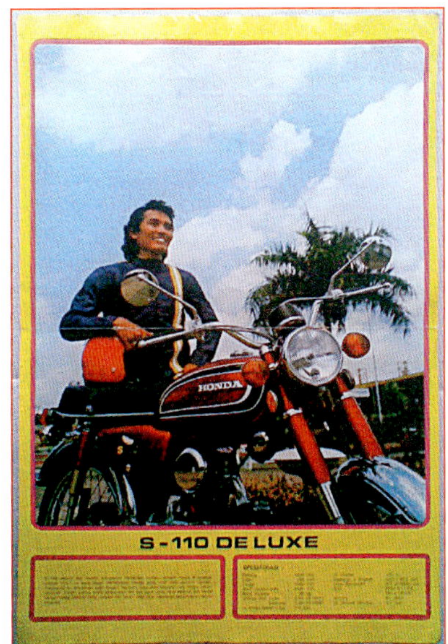

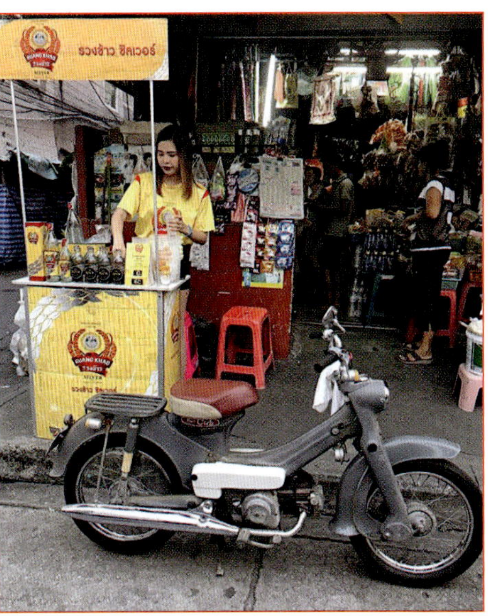

The S 110 and C 240 Port Cub were reserved for the Asian market only. These vehicles had OHV engines and were designed purely as work-horses for everyday use.

The unconventional CT 50 Motra has parking brakes and a fuel gauge directly in front of the seat. It could pass for a military cross between the CY and ST. The engine with three-speed transmission even received a special housing for the reduction box.

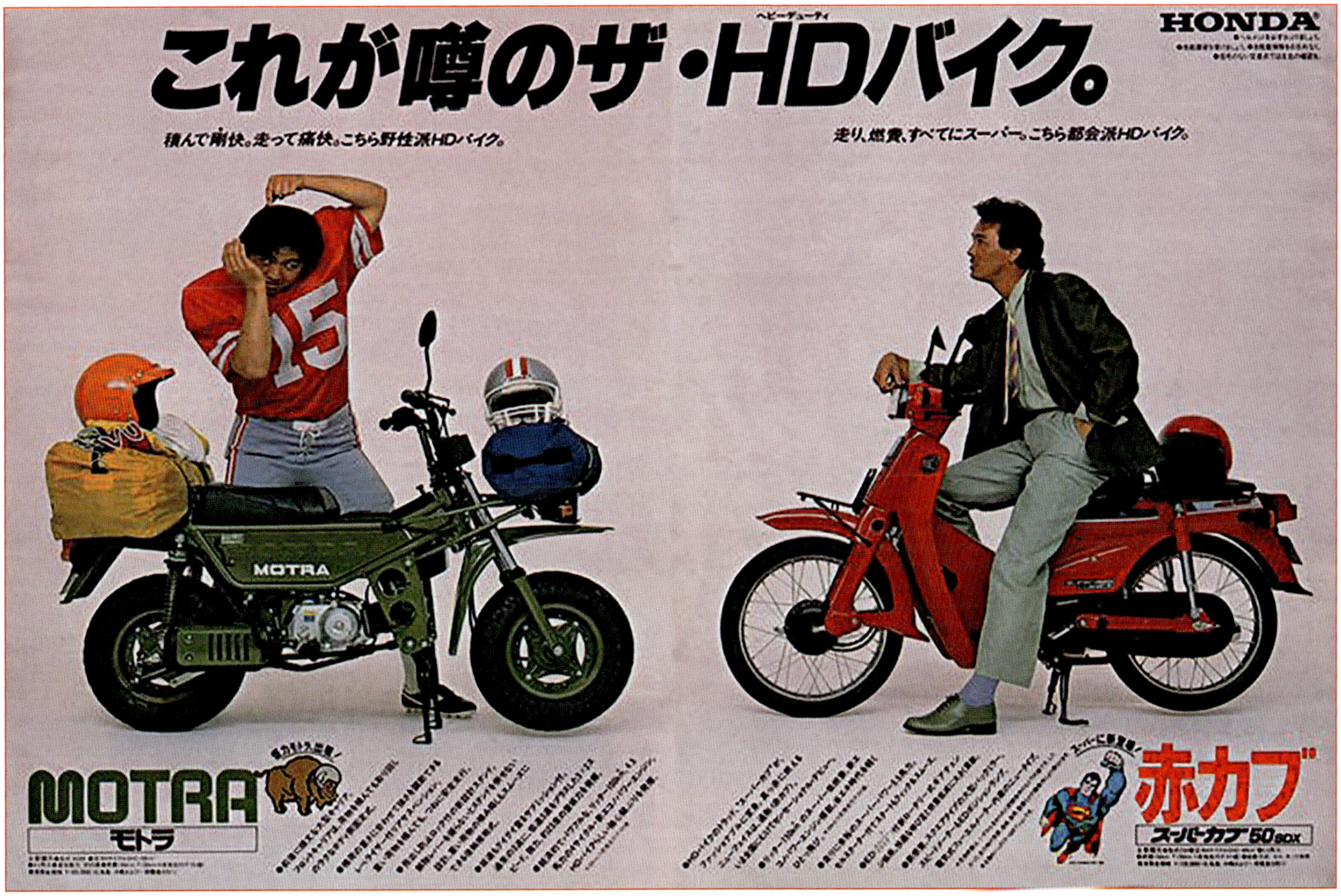
HONDA
ヘビーデューティ
これが噂のザ・HDバイク。
積んで剛快。走って痛快。こちら野性派HDバイク。
走り、燃費、すべてにスーパー。こちら都会派HDバイク。
MOTRA
MOTRA
モトラ
赤カブ
スーパーカブ50 BOX

EXOTIC ASIAN: HONDA C 240 PORT CUB

Why did Honda's marketing manager Takeo Fujisawa come up with the idea of building yet another simplified light version of the Super Cub in the early 1960s? He surely saw an export market (the C 100 was quickly successful in Vietnam)—a market for customers who wanted to ride something even simpler and, above all, even lighter. Three gears were too many; the engine also needed to be simpler and more reliable, and certain components need to be more accessible and easier to replace.

A new type of engine was designed for the C 240 Port Cub, which incorporated some elements of the C 100 unit but had parallel valves for ease of maintenance—as in a '98 Gilera or Moto Guzzi's first Stornello version. Likewise, two gears were enough for the "Cub Light" instead of the three-speed transmission. With 2.3 hp at 5,700 rpm instead of the C 100's 4.5 hp, the Port Cub managed about 31 mph (50 kph). With an unladen weight of 117 pounds (53 kg), it was predestined for women—the only known advertising brochure shows almost exclusively ladies using their Port Cubs, not as work vehicles but as a leisure machines.

Instead of the closed leg shield, no plastic leg protection was initially added; only when the designation "Port Cub" was replaced by "Cub Light" did this slimmed-down version receive leg protection, but here with more openings, as well as with side covers open at the bottom instead of the oval, closed versions of the Super Cub.

Climbing ability was quoted at 12 percent and the price at 43,000 yen. An interesting feature of the engine is that here the fixed kick-starter without a folding mechanism does not emerge from the right side of the housing but sits directly behind the gearshift lever. The long boom of the muffler bracket was also fitted to an early C 100, but it was soon replaced by a more stable and less resonant one. The C 240 was built for only two years—and never offered in Europe. A handful of examples do exist—at least one in England. It was acquired by a soldier stationed in Singapore who returned with it to England in 1967.

Of interest is the fact that the C 240 probably formed the basis for the C 310 A built in Aalst. When the Port Cub was discontinued in Japan, production of the manually shifted 50s began in Belgium. Many parts, as the spare parts catalog of the pedal version shows, even still have the code of the previous C 240. If you are looking for one, you should look around in Vietnam; that's also where most of the owners active in the C 240 Port Cub Facebook group can be found.

The C 240 Port Cub, also called Honda 50 light, had a round speedometer, no handlebar fairing, and just two gears. The repro dial has errors: 1,400 rpm can never correspond to 60 kph (37.2 mph).

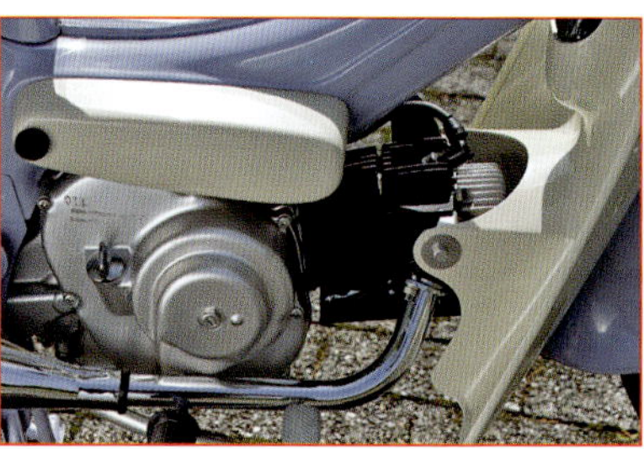

Some parts of the C 240 engine were used in Aalst for the C 310. The kick-starter was not found on the right side behind the clutch, but rather it was on the opposite side behind the gearshift lever.

INTENDED EXCLUSIVELY FOR ROUGH GOING: HONDA CT 50 MOTRA

A full 23 degrees of climbing ability thanks to its dual-range transmission – this made the Motra from 1982 a 50 that you could confidently use on an expedition. Due to its boxy appearance, it was not built for the 50 cc market but was actually intended only for special customers in Japan itself. Therefore, advertising can be found only in Japanese. Here is the translation of the Japanese press release:

> The Honda Motra is equipped with a variety of equipment to fully enjoy the outdoor life – for example, a large luggage rack for a variety of tools.
>
> The engine is equipped with a four-stroke Econopower engine (air-cooled, 49 cc single cylinder producing 4.5 hp), which is known for its toughness and durability. In addition, it is equipped with a transmission that adds three low gears to the normal third gear. Use of the dual-range transmission ensures pronounced climbing capabilities even when carrying luggage and in mountainous terrain.

A pack mule for off-road use, the CT 50 Motra was available in yellow or green. It can only be found in Japan.

The boxy Motra rides much more ponderously than its siblings, but thanks to the main stand, which is hinged far forward, it stands absolutely straight.

The maximum payload of this 50 cc motorcycle is up to 30 kg (66 pounds).

The redesigned main stand, located in the front of the frame, has a locking mechanism and is designed to operate the stand safely without pulling the release lever on the left handlebar. The styling emphasizes the image of a wild outdoor motorcycle with a cargo rack and solid frame. This will make the 50 cc Honda vehicles a complete series with seven models and ten types. A total of 45 000 vehicles are to be sold per year. The standard cash price is 165,000 yen (prices for Hokkaido and Okinawa are 3,000 yen higher, except for some remote islands).

Since the C 240 Port Cub was even lighter than the C 100 at 53 kg, it was predestined for use as a pure transport aid for daily shopping. As a sporty version of the last OHV models, the modified C 200 OHV engine was installed in the more modern S 110 chassis from 1973.

Equipped with a large luggage carrier and a sturdy tubular frame, the Motra can be fully loaded front and rear. In particular, the front carrier attached to the frame is said to ensure stable maneuverability even when carrying luggage.

In addition, the suspension can be fine-tuned according to the weight of the luggage and the condition of the road. An indicator on the rear suspension allows the respective setting to be seen at a glance. The wide tires with block tread allow the loading of heavy luggage. You can enjoy a stable ride.

MAIN FEATURES

Air-cooled, 49 cc, single-cylinder 4.5 hp engine, featuring economy and durability. High-low range shifting is a one-touch lever operation, equipped with a cargo rack on a sturdy tubular frame that can be fully loaded. Rear suspension with leveling device allows you to adjust the shock absorber to the weight and condition of the road and see the adjustment position at a glance. A newly designed stand with locking mechanism at the front.

Technical data:	L × W × H (mm) 1655 × 740 × 975
Wheelbase (mm)	1,125
Dry weight (kg)	76
Seat height (mm)	720
Frame shape	Backbone
Tire size	5.40-10-4 PR
Engine type	AD05E
Caster (mm)	27° 00/44
Maximum power (hp/rpm)	4.5/7500
Compression ratio	9.8
Ignition method	CDI
Fuel tank capacity (L)	4.5
Gear ratio	1. 3.272/1.823/1.190
Dual-range transmission	1.459
Carburetor model	PB59
Battery	6V-2AH

A strange, elaborate combination of old and new, the S 110 top end is reminiscent of the C 100, the round air filter of the ST 70. Only on this engine is the oil filler neck on the left, and only the S 110 has an additional sight glass, visible above the gearshift lever.

HONDA S 110 BENLY

Between 1973 and 1976, the S 110 Benly was built in Thailand and also sold in Australia. It is powered by a modified, very robust C 200 engine with OHV control and four-speed transmission in an S 90 chassis. The oil filler neck is on the left in front of the gearshift rocker; there is also a sight glass for a visual check of the oil level. The S 110 engine is thus the only horizontal four-stroke single in the entire Honda series where the dipstick does not have to be pulled out to check the oil level; it's an interesting mixture of horizontal C 200 engine concept with some ideas from the later CG series, which replaced the S 110 from 1976 onward.

HONDA
FUV
823J

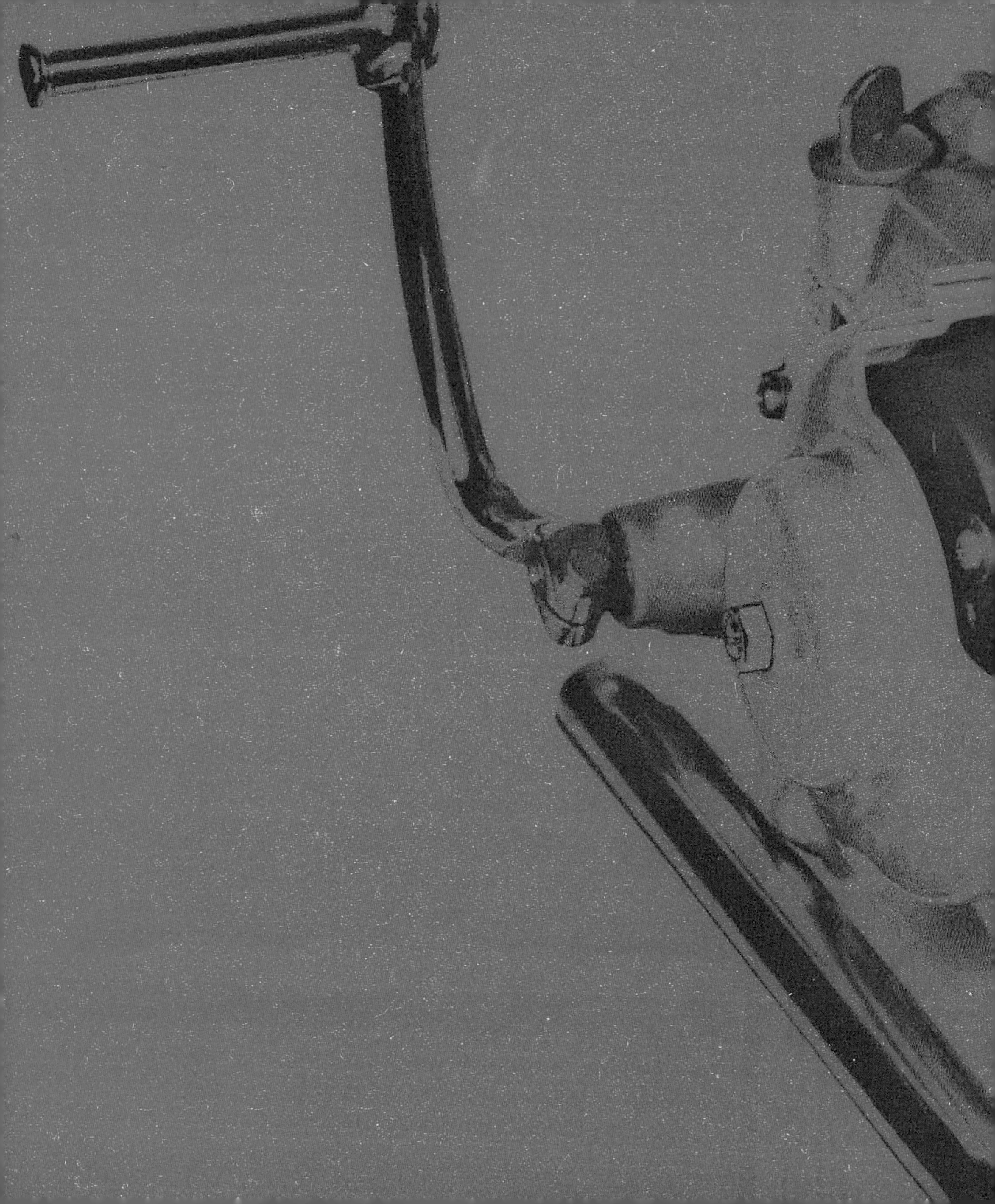